Vera
Lex

Journal of the International Natural Law Society

New Series Volume 8, Numbers 1&2   Winter 2007

CONTRIBUTORS

Address all submissions and correspondence to The Editor, VERA LEX, Pace University, Department of Philosophy & Religious Studies, 1 Pace Plaza, New York, NY 10038. Please send two copies of the paper submitted. Include adequate margins, double space everything (text, notes, works cited, quotations). Use U.S. spelling and punctuation style, (e.g. periods inside quotation marks; "double quotes" for opening and closing quotations). The University of Chicago Manual of Style, 13th Edition, is to be consulted regarding matters of style. Notes are to be numbered consecutively (in Arabic numerals) and placed at the bottom of the page.

SUBSCRIBERS
VERA LEX is published annually by Pace University Press, 41 Park Row, Room 1510, New York, NY 10038. Subscription price: $40. Please send all subscription inquiries to: PaceUP@services.pace.edu

INDEXING AND ABSTRACTING
VERA LEX is indexed in *Philosopher's Index.*

VERA LEX, the journal of the International Natural Law Society, was established to communicate and dialogue on the subject of natural law and natural right, to introduce natural law philosophy into the mainstream of contemporary thought, and to strengthen the current revived interest in the discussion of morals and law and advance its historical research.

Why do we use a shell (*Nautilus pomplilus Linnaeus*) to symbolize *vera lex*? The logarithmic spiraling and overlapping chambers of the shell are endless. They suggest a patterned development and evolution that, by its radial and circular design, never comes to an end. This means that the shell is at once specific and real, while its form, like law, is abstract and ideal.

The pattern of a shell is, like good law, uniform, regular and reliable. It can therefore be anticipated and known. The pattern of a shell is balanced, like justice. *Una iustitia.*

A shell is a biological being. Like law, it has life and dynamic. It grows. (There is an average of thirty growth lines per chamber, one for every day in the lunar cycle, suggesting that a new chamber is put down each lunar month and a new growth line each day, thus recording two different natural rhythms, lunar and solar.)

The shell is a universal and common object known to everyone. A shell is not soft tissue easily destroyed. And yet, like liberty, it is fragile in certain respects if stepped on with an iron boot. It has to be guarded with vigilance or it is crushed.

In every shell lives a nautilus. If the shell is law, the nautilus (snail) is a person—it is alive—person and law. Their destinies, like person and law, are interdependent.

Vera
Lex
leges innumerae, una iustitia

CONTENTS

NEW SERIES VOLUME 8, NUMBERS 1 & 2   WINTER 2007

FEATURED ARTICLES

FEATURED ARTICLES

THE MORALITY OF THE EIGHTH AMENDMENT: CRUELTY, DIGNITY, AND NATURAL RIGHTS

Jacob M. Held

> *Capital punishments are the natural offspring of monarchical governments . . . Kings consider their subjects as their property; no wonder, therefore, they shed their blood with as little emotion as men shed the blood of their sheep or cattle. But the principles of republican governments speak a very different language . . . An execution in a republic is like a human sacrifice in religion.*[1]

What follows is an exploration into the meaning of the Eighth Amendment, specifically the prohibition on "Cruel and Unusual" punishments. The Eighth Amendment is unique insofar as it is expressed in moral terms. As such, it must be interpreted in moral language and through moral argument. But using moral language to adjudicate cases regarding fundamental liberties or limits on state and federal power is problematic. A moral approach to constitutional interpretation raises the specter of natural law, while requiring the use of vague moral language and moral argumentation to delineate a sphere of protected liberty. In addition, moral arguments give the appearance of subjectivity, preference, or mere opinion and seem to put judges in the position—as Judge Learned Hand once remarked—of Platonic Guardians.[2] But as a statement of natural, moral rights couched in moral language the Eighth Amendment must be parsed out lest it be thrown into the dustbin of history as a relic; an antiquated statement of human dignity and natural rights written by quaint natural lawyers. I contend that the Eighth Amendment must be read morally and that a moral reading of the Eighth Amendment emphasizes

---

[1] Benjamin Rush, quoted in David J. Rothman, "Perfecting the Prison: United States, 1789–1865," Chap. 4 in *The Oxford History of the Prison: The Practice of Punishment in Western Society*, ed. Norval Morris and David J. Rothman (New York: Oxford University Press., 1998), 102.

[2] Cf. Learned Hand, *The Bill of Rights: The Oliver Wendell Holmes Lectures*, 1958 (Cambridge: Harvard University Press, 1958), 73.

the importance of a moral interpretive framework for understanding the Constitution as a moral document expressing the existence of natural, moral rights. In fact, a moral interpretation is truly originalist insofar as it captures the original intent of the Framers and the original meaning of the clauses.

This article is divided into three parts. The first part deals primarily with the case law surrounding the Eighth Amendment, primarily *Gregg v. Georgia* (1976). The second part deals with the Eighth Amendment in isolation in an attempt to demonstrate that it does in fact make moral claims and must be read morally in a natural rights context. This section also focuses on a moral interpretive schema for the Constitution and the Bill of Rights generally, although directed mostly towards the Eighth Amendment. In conclusion, I will present the case that a moral reading of the Eighth Amendment justifies Justice William Brennan's contention that capital punishment is in all cases unconstitutional and has a profound impact on an assessment of American penal practices generally. I will begin with a look at how the Eighth Amendment has been read in the past.

I. GREGG V. GEORGIA

In the majority opinion of *Gregg v. Georgia* (1976) the court ruled not only that the case under consideration did not violate the Eighth or Fourteenth Amendments, but that the death penalty was not *per se* a violation of the Eighth Amendment, that is, capital punishment is not in itself cruel and unusual. Justice Stewart writes: "We now hold that the penalty of death does not invariably violate the Constitution."[3] The majority opinion includes several arguments for the permissibility of capital punishment reliant on various moral conceptions of cruelty. The majority opinion states:

> The Eighth Amendment, which has been interpreted in a flexible and dynamic manner in accord with the evolving standards of decency, forbids the use of punishment that is "excessive" either because it involves the unnecessary and wanton infliction of pain or because it is grossly disproportionate to the severity of the crime.[4]

[3] *Gregg v. Georgia*, 428 U.S. 169 (1976).

[4] Ibid., at 154.

Citing *Weems v. U.S.* (1910) for the precedent on proportionality and *Wilkerkson v. Utah* (1879) with respect to excessiveness, as well as other cases, the majority concluded that the Eighth Amendment is a prohibition on excessive or gratuitous suffering and death as a punishment does not in itself pass this threshold.[5] Thus, in determining the meaning of the term "cruel," the majority declared that "cruel" is synonymous with "excessive" or "unnecessary" suffering. In an attempt to make more precise the vague moral term "cruel" the majority, looking to precedent, does so with reference to supposedly less morally charged language, namely, with reference to empirically or objectively determinable conditions such as excessiveness or superfluity.

In addition, the majority maintained that capital punishment was accepted by the Framers of the Constitution so any reading that is to remain true to the text and original meaning cannot find the Eighth Amendment to prohibit capital punishment, that is, if the death penalty was not cruel to those who drafted the Eighth, then it cannot be cruel now. The majority held:

> It is apparent from the text of the Constitution itself that the existence of capital punishment was accepted by the Framers. At the time the Eighth Amendment was ratified, capital punishment was a common sanction in every State. Indeed, the First Congress of the United States enacted legislation providing death as the penalty for specified crimes. C. 9, 1 Stat. 112 (1790). The Fifth Amendment, adopted at the same time as the Eighth, contemplated the continued existence of the capital sanction by imposing certain limits on the prosecution of capital cases . . . [6]

The above argument relies on an implied originalist reading that demands that the expectations of the Framers, that is, their beliefs about how a clause should be enforced are binding and exhaust the original meaning of the text. However, as will be demonstrated below, as a moral clause the

---

[5] Cf. *Weems v. U.S.* 217 U..S. 349 (1910); *Wilkerson v. Utah* 99 U.S. 130 (1879). For subsequent uses of the same or similar criteria see: *Harmelin v. Michigan* 501 U.S. 957 (1991) where the Eighth Amendment is declared to include a general rule of proportionality; *Coker v. Georgia* 433 U.S. 584 (1977) and *Enmund v. Florida* 458 U.S. 782 (1982) where excessiveness is a criterion.

[6] *Gregg v. Georgia*, 428 U.S. 177 (1976); This argument is also made in *Roberts v. Louisiana* 428 U.S. 325 (1976) (White, J. dissenting).

Eighth Amendment is prone to misinterpretations and misapplications such that it is not only possible, but plausible that the Framers were themselves mistaken in believing certain punishments not to be cruel.

The majority continues by proffering the argument that the death penalty is the expressed will of the people as reflected through their representatives in state and federal legislatures. With reference to Chief Justice Earl Warren's famous dictum from *Trop v. Dulles* (1958), the court concurred that the Eighth Amendment "must draw its meaning from the evolving standards of decency that mark the progress of a maturing society."[7] The majority herein accepts that the Eighth Amendment is imprecise and must draw its meaning from prevailing moral sentiment. That is, "cruel" means what current prevailing moral sentiment declares it means. They are quick to add, however, that this does not imply that the meaning of the Eighth Amendment is subjectively determined. Rather, "it requires that we look to objective indicia that reflect the public attitude toward a given sanction."[8] But even if the American public supports the death penalty and does not find it to be cruel, this does not settle the matter. For, if the Eighth Amendment is a moral clause that reflects an absolute value, then prevailing moral sentiment is irrelevant insofar as the truth of the matter is determined without reference to public opinion. Yet, the majority appears to be claiming that the meaning of cruelty changes with the winds of public sentiment. In addition to the claim that "cruel" means what the people believe it means, there is also the implicit claim that the court must defer to the will of the people, that is, for the court to overrule publicly accepted legislation on doubtful moral grounds is for it to behave undemocratically.

> Therefore, in assessing a punishment selected by a democratically elected legislature against a constitutional measure, we presume its validity. We may not require the legislature to select the least severe penalty possible so long as the penalty selected is not cruelly inhumane or disproportionate to the crime involved. And a heavy burden rests on those who would attack the judgment of the representatives of the people.[9]

---

[7] *Trop v. Dulles* 356 U.S. 86 (1958), also cited in *Gregg v. Georgia*, 428 U.S. 153 (1976).

[8] *Gregg v. Georgia*, 428 U.S. 173 (1976).

[9] Ibid., at 175.

The majority of the court is reflecting in this statement a concern for the separation of powers. Namely, the will of the people as reflected through their representatives in state and federal legislatures should be presumed legitimate unless a compelling case can be made to the contrary. In the case of the death penalty, if the people want it and their legislatures accommodate them, then the burden of proof lies on the courts to demonstrate that the public and their democratically elected officials are in error. Only then can their democratically manifested will be overturned by unelected judges and their ostensibly idiosyncratic understanding of cruelty.

Finally, the majority opinion maintains that capital punishment is morally permissible and perhaps even demanded insofar as it fits both retributive and deterrent theories of punishment.[10] This may be true, but as will be demonstrated below, probably irrelevant. In presenting all of these arguments the majority may be seen as offering what they take to be a thorough refutation of the constitutionally based abolitionist argument. To dismiss the text, Framers' intent, precedent, common political morality, and accepted moral traditions is an egregious case of judicial activism based in doubtful moral argument. The majority is in effect claiming that there is no interpretive schema that can hold that the death penalty is unconstitutional, even though their own interpretation and application of "cruel" relies upon similar claims and arguments.

Dissenting Justice William J. Brennan Jr. offers an alternative reading of the cruel and unusual punishments clause. Justice Brennan, in agreement with Chief Justice Earl Warren's opinion in *Trop v. Dulles*, affirms that the Eighth Amendment is fundamentally a statement of moral principle; one that affirms and reiterates the importance of human dignity, or as Chief Justice Warren states, "The basic concept underlying the Eighth Amendment is nothing less than the dignity of man."[11] Citing Justice Brennan's concurring opinion in *Furman v. Georgia*:

> At bottom . . . the Cruel and Unusual Punishments Clause prohibits the infliction of uncivilized and *inhuman* punishments. The State, even as it punishes, must treat its members with respect for their *intrinsic worth* as human

[10] Ibid., at 183-4. See also *Roberts v. Louisiana* 428 U.S 325 (1976) (White, J. dissenting) and *Furman v. Georgia* 408 U.S. 238 (1972) (Burger, J. dissenting) for retributivist and deterrence claims.

[11] See *Trop v. Dulles* 356 U.S. 100 (1958).

> beings. A punishment is "cruel and unusual," therefore, if
> it does not comport with *human dignity*.[12]

Likewise, in reference to why certain punishments such as the rack and thumbscrews are prohibited he continues, "The true significance of these punishments is that they treat members of the human race as nonhumans, as objects to be toyed with and discarded."[13] According to Justice Brennan, the Eighth Amendment is a statement of moral principle; it is about the inherent dignity of humankind and since the punishment of death is a violation of human dignity in all instances it is unconstitutional in all cases.

Justice Brennan, arguably, is a natural lawyer. He envisions the Constitution as expressing political and moral principles. He states: "the Founding Fathers knew better than to pin down their descendents too closely. Enduring principles rather than petty details were what they sought to write down."[14] Brennan takes these principles to be about the dignity of the human being and a check on the federal government restricting how it may treat its citizens.[15] In this regard, Brennan correctly reflects the intent behind the addition of a Bill of Rights, namely, the protection of natural rights from a possibly tyrannical federal government. This was the concern of the anti-federalists and the worry James Madison hoped to assuage through the addition of a Bill of Rights. The Eighth Amendment must be read respectful of this tradition. According to Justice Brennan, the role of a justice is to test the law against these principles when its legal basis is doubtful. What is paramount is remaining true to the principles laid out in the document. Namely, the protection of natural rights whose function is the protection of those interests vital to human beings insofar as they are rational moral beings. The principle of the Eighth Amendment is about maintaining respect for the inherent human dignity of all people, and it is this inherent moral worth that binds the government, even as it punishes. Whatsoever disparages this absolute

---

[12] *Furman v. Georgia*, 408 U.S. 270 (1972) (Brennan, J., concurring) (my emphasis).

[13] Ibid., at 272-273.

[14] William J. Brennan Jr., *An Affair with Freedom: A Collection of His Opinions and Speeches Drawn from His First Decade as a United States Supreme Court Justice*, ed. Stephen J. Friedman (New York: Atheneum, 1967), 324.

[15] Cf. William J. Brennan Jr., "The Constitution of the United States: Contemporary Ratification," in *Judges on Judging: Views from the Bench*, ed. David M. O'Brien (Washington, D.C.: CQ Press, 2004), 183-193.

value is as a consequence an illegitimate use of power. But before this line of reasoning is investigated further, it ought to be emphasized why "cruelty" is the operative concept in the Eighth Amendment, and not oddity or the "unusual" nature of the punishment. Such a discussion is necessary in order to elucidate why the Eighth Amendment can only be understood as a moral clause, and why it is paramount to discern its moral meaning.

II. "CRUEL AND UNUSUAL": THE ORIGINAL MEANING

Let us begin with the text of the Eighth Amendment. One could read the "and" in the cruel and unusual punishments clause in two ways. The first way would be to read it as an "or," that is, the Eighth Amendment is a prohibition on cruel punishments and unusual punishments such that the constitutionality of a punishment relies on whether it meets one or both of these criteria. In this sense, the "and" functions as a disjunct; if a punishment is cruel or unusual it is unconstitutional, where the "or" is inclusive. Thus, effectively the clause would read: "Nor cruel or unusual punishments inflicted." Another way of reading the "and" is as a strict conjunction such that a punishment must be both cruel and unusual before it can be rendered unconstitutional.

A. Cruel or *Unusual*

In practice, the majority of Eighth Amendment cases that address whether the penalty of death is *per se* a violation of the prohibition on cruel and unusual punishments tend to focus solely on cruelty. That is, they ask whether a punishment is excessively harsh, unnecessary, or offensive to human dignity, and other questions that would be relevant to determining whether a punishment were cruel. Never do such arguments rely on the oddity of the punishment. In actuality, the conjunction is read as a disjunction. If a punishment is cruel, that is sufficient to classify it as unconstitutional; it does not need also to be unusual. But, oddly enough, if a punishment is unusual this appears to be neither sufficient nor necessary. That is, a punishment's odd nature is not enough to classify it as unconstitutional and cruel punishments can be perfectly common and still rendered unconstitutional. In actual decisions, "unusual" seems irrelevant. But David Hershenov has offered an account for why "unusual" is relevant to the Eighth Amendment and why the Eighth must be read as a strict conjunction.

In his article, "Why Must Punishment Be Unusual as Well as Cruel to Be Unconstitutional?" Hershenov begins with the idea that the Constitution ought to be read according to an originalist interpretation, so the text of the Eighth Amendment should be read literally and with respect to the intent and expectation of the Framers.[16] Regarding the wording of the Eighth Amendment, however, its genealogy is less helpful than one would hope. Anthony Granucci's oft-referenced piece, "'Nor Cruel and Unusual Punishments Inflicted:' The Original Meaning" is considered the authoritative account.[17] Granucci traces the lineage of the Eighth Amendment back from its finished form to its origin. As it appears in the Bill of Rights, the Eighth Amendment is a verbatim copy of a clause in Virginia's Declaration of Rights of 1776 drafted by George Mason, and this is a verbatim copy of a similar clause in the English Bill of Rights of 1689. However, the English Bill of Rights, although it does include a prohibition on cruel and unusual punishments, sheds little light on the meaning of the text as the Eighth Amendment. With respect to the history of the clause in the English Bill of Rights, Granucci notes that it morphed from "illegal punishments" to "illegal and cruel punishments," and finally to "cruel and unusual punishments." He concludes, "The final phraseology, especially the use of the word 'unusual,' must be laid simply to chance and sloppy draftsmanship."[18] If this word truly is a mistake, then to give it any weight simply out of deference to its origin would be to give credence to an error. This bit of historical trivia raises an important point with respect to originalism: questions regarding the origin of a text are mostly matters of historical curiosity, not of philosophical importance since textual heredity tells you only where the words came from and not necessarily what they mean or were understood to mean. After all, it is not a matter of what the word meant to the English in 1689 or why the English chose to adopt such a prohibition, but why the Framers chose to adopt it, that is, what meaning they imparted to it. The only way to arrive at this original meaning of the Eighth Amendment—the meaning of the Framers—is to look at the debates surrounding it as well as contemporaneous uses of the concepts of cruel and unusual, as well as the ostensible purpose of the clause, a process Hershenov regretably foregoes.

---

[16] David B. Hershenov, "Why Must Punishment be Unusual as Well as Cruel to be Unconstitutional?" *Public Affairs Quarterly*, Vol. 16, no. 1 (Jan. 2002), 77-98.

[17] Cf. Anthony F. Granucci, "'Nor Cruel and Unusual Punishments Inflicted:' The Original Meaning," *California Law Review*, Vol. 57, no. 4 (Oct. 1969), 839-865.

[18] Ibid., 855.

The history of the Eighth Amendment, as relevant to the current undertaking, begins in the Continental Congress. When the original compact was offered to the original states it contained in it the Second Article which read in part "and no cruel or unusual punishments shall be inflicted."[19] This is one of, if not the, earliest mentions of a prohibition on cruel punishments in American constitutional law and it is clear in this case that cruel and unusual operate distinctly from each other as indicated by the "or." This phenomenon is repeated other places as well. When the House and Senate debated amending the Constitution the Eighth Amendment was originally the Tenth Article. In the congressional record, however, the Tenth Article is in at least two places cited as a prohibition on "cruel or unusual" punishments. It is quoted as "nor cruel or unusual punishments" by the constituencies from both New York and Rhode Island.[20] This point need not be overemphasized, but it does speak to a relevant interpretative issue. That the "or" occurs in several spots is suggestive of the mindset regarding the clause; cruel punishments and unusual punishments are morally repugnant and ought to be prohibited. Regarding the independence of cruel from unusual punishments, consider the attitude of Patrick Henry. When considering the issue of punishments Henry asks, "When a person shall be treated in the most horrid manner, and most cruelly and inhumanly tortured, will the security of territorial rights grant him redress?"[21] Henry sees a prohibition on cruelty to be fundamental and to operate separately from any prohibition on unusual punishments. The record suggests that cruelty does operate separately from oddity in constitutional matters. One could ask, if cruel were truly enough to cover the intent of the Framers and express their original meaning, then what does "unusual" bring to the Eighth Amendment, that is, why would it have been perceived to be a worthy addition?

Patrick Henry, in the same exchange referenced above, expresses his opinion that unusual punishments are themselves problematic, although he appears to be alone in this.[22] So he not only severs the connection between

[19] *Journals of the Continental Congress 1774–1789*, ed. Worthington C. Ford et al. (Washington D.C., 1904–37), 22:340.

[20] 1 *Annals of Congress* 2035 (Joseph Gales, ed. 1790) and *Senate Journal*. 1st Cong., 2nd Sess. 16 June 1790, 159. (Respectively.)

[21] 3 *The Debates in the Several State Conventions on the Adoption of the Federal Constitution* 512 (Jonathan Elliot ed., 2nd ed. 1907) [Herein after: *Elliot's Debates*].

[22] Ibid.

cruel and unusual but also thinks unusual to be a sufficient criterion to morally condemn a punishment. Hershenov would seem to agree. He argues: if the Framers were under the impression that the system of government they instituted was for the most part just, then they would be wary of allowing major deviations from an already just system.[23] Prohibiting unusual punishments would constrain judges and legislatures from veering too far afield from the already just punishments in practice. This seems to be the idea Henry is intimating. "Unusual" serves as a "quasi-statistical" check on punishment. In addition, the fact that the Amendment is actually written as a conjunction militates against dismissal of the "unusual" aspect of the clause, that is, we must presume that the Framers included an "and" intentionally and we should be concerned about why they would do so. But Hershenov's understanding of the "and" is implausible given the record. The problem with emphasizing the relevance of "unusual" is that as far as the record shows Patrick Henry was the only one who thought the clause that would become the Eighth Amendment was about anything other than purely cruel punishments. With reference to what would become the Eighth Amendment, Governor Randolph refers to a prohibition on "cruel punishments,"[24] and President of the Virginia convention, Edmund Pendleton likewise refers only to "cruel punishment."[25] The record is far from extensive since the Eighth Amendment never seemed to engender great debate, but the evidence that exists is suggestive of a disjunction between cruel and unusual, and the fact that cruelty was meant to be the operative concept, not oddity. The language of the Eighth Amendment was adopted for the purpose of prohibiting governmental abuse of citizens through a restriction on how it could punish, namely, in a humane or non-cruel manner. Thus, in order to understand the meaning of the Eighth Amendment one must divine the meaning of cruelty as understood by the Framers and ratifiers of the Amendment.

B. *The Original Meaning of "Cruel"*

Hershenov, relying on his spurious interpretation of the Eighth Amendment, makes the following claim: "cruel" is merely descriptive, that is, it means "harsh." According to Hershenov, cruelty is not an inherently evaluative concept. It is not the case that if something is cruel

[23] Cf. Hershenov, "Why Must Punishment be Unusual as Well as Cruel to be Unconstitutional?" 82.

[24] 3 *Elliot's Debates* 468.

[25] Ibid., 294.

it is in virtue of this fact morally repugnant. He states: "Something can be cruel without deserving moral condemnation."[26] Cruelty is synonymous with harshness, and harshness alone is not morally offensive. This explains his belief that "unusual" must be read literally and included in any interpretative schema. If "harsh" is merely descriptive, then being harsh cannot be sufficient to constitute a punishment's being offensive and so unconstitutional. Something must be both cruel, that is harsh, and unusual, that is unjust, in order to violate the Eighth Amendment. In not finding cruelty to be morally offensive, Hershenov appears to be a kindred spirit of New Hampshire Representative Samuel Livermore, whom he invokes in support of his argument. Although, as noted below, whereas Hershenov maintains that cruel is a non-evaluative term, Livermore uses it in the common sense of brutal, inhuman, or tortuous and still finds such punishments acceptable.

Livermore argued against George Mason and Patrick Henry and the ratification of the Eighth Amendment claiming that we may in fact need cruel punishments. Livermore states: "It is sometimes necessary to hang a man, villains often deserve whipping, and perhaps having their ears cut off; but are we in the future to be prevented from inflicting these punishments because they are cruel?"[27] Some have understood Livermore here to be arguing that harsh penalties are sometimes deserved or necessitated by the crime or circumstance. His statements are taken as proof that cruel must be understood as merely harsh in a purely descriptive way and not the morally charged notion of inhuman or gratuitously abusive. After all, who would propose that barbarous punishments are ever deserved, or that we are justified in using tortuous methods of punishment? But on a strict deterrence theory of punishment barbarity might be deemed necessary or most expedient. Today some still argue for the use of notably cruel practices such as torture if they prove effective. On some retributive theories, stricter *lex talionis* models, one might deserve to be treated inhumanely if one ceded one's status as a full fledged member of the moral community through the commission of a truly heinous crime. Livermore's statements are consistent with the attitude that cruel does not simply mean harsh. It would be perfectly reasonable to read Livermore as arguing not that we should be allowed to use strict or harsh means of

---

[26] Hershenov, "Why Must Punishment be Unusual as Well as Cruel to be Unconstitutional?" 78.

[27] 1 *Annals of Congress* 782-783 (Joseph Gales, ed. 1790); also cited in *Furman v. Georgia*, 408 U.S. 262 (1972).

punishing criminal offenders, but that we need to leave open the possibility of using inhuman practices, such as ear cropping or branding, since they might be necessary or even deserved, practices a moral idea of cruelty would forbid. Thus, for Livermore the ban on cruel punishments might be too great a restriction on governmental power. The government, it could be argued, requires flexibility in its capacity to punish in order to provide security and since the Eighth Amendment is inflexible in its prohibition of cruel or inhumane treatment it is too restrictive. This line of reasoning expresses the fear that the Eighth Amendment too greatly limits what punishments are acceptable. Livermore, arguably, is communicating this concern because he understood what the Eighth Amendment said: morally repugnant practices are disallowed. Not only is attributing this position to Livermore fair, but it appears demanded given the common usage and understanding of the term "cruel" at the time and the proposed purpose of the ban on cruel punishments.

Ultimately, if we want to know what Livermore meant by "cruel" we merely need to look at how the word functioned during his time. In the record there are several instructive instances of the use of the term. First, Patrick Henry pairs up cruel with other morally evaluative concepts such as in his pairing "cruelly and inhumanly tortured."[28] Secondly, Edmund Pendelton refers to cruel punishments "such as tortures, inquisitions, and the like—shocking to human nature, and only calculated to coerce the dominion of tyrants over slaves."[29] Truly telling is Maryland Representative Michael Jenifer Stone's remarks regarding a bill proposing the use of deceased prisoners for experimental surgery: The proposal "was making punishment wear the appearance of cruelty."[30] What is suggested by these uses of "cruelty" is not surprising. Just as nowadays, cruelty is a moral concept connoting repugnant, offensive, and inhumane treatment of moral agents. After all, how could dissecting deceased prisoners appear cruel if cruel meant harsh? The English language simply has not changed that much since the framing, and since cruelty is used today in a moral context, it should not be surprising that it was used similarly during the framing and ratification of the Eighth Amendment. Thus, Livermore's case is for the permissibility of inhumane punishments, that is, cruel punishments and not supportive of

---

[28] 3 *Elliot's Debates* 512.

[29] Ibid., 468.

[30] *U.S. House Journal*. 1790 1st Cong., 2nd Sess., 6 April. 1572.

Hershenov's contention that cruel is now or was in the past synonymous with a merely descriptive term such as harsh.

Hershenov seems concerned, as are many who consider the scope of judicial review and constitutional interpretation, with preventing "activist" judges from interpreting more into the Eighth Amendment than can reasonably be so read. He sees disregard of the "unusual" half of the clause as well as a moral reading of "cruel" to be the way activists often justify their interpretations of the Eighth Amendment. But Hershenov's case is weak. The "unusual" half of the clause seems to be superfluous, which even if taken as a serious addition, in no way impacts the meaning of cruelty which is itself sufficient to render a punishment unconstitutional. A brief survey of the relevant debates proves this point. The Eighth Amendment was not a prohibition on strict punishments; it was and still is a prohibition on inhuman, tortuous, and barbarous ones. Hershenov wants to read the Eighth Amendment as descriptive, not morally evaluative, in an attempt to remove judicial discretion, thus demanding that as descriptive it be parsed out in purely non-moral terminology as though the adjudication of Eighth Amendment cases could be a deductive matter. But this reading of the Eighth is contrary to its origins, meaning, and intent, and it threatens to disparage the very protections the Eighth was drafted to guarantee.

The problem of the Eighth Amendment is that the wording is vague in virtue of being moral. What specifically is cruel is not easily discernible. In fact, some would claim that it has no meaning outside of popular opinion or consensus thus claiming that it is culturally relative or even subjective. But its meaning is discernible from its origins in the natural rights tradition of the Framers.

C. The Eighth Amendment and Natural Rights

The Framers' intent in adopting the Bill of Rights was to safeguard the natural, moral rights of the people and promote clear principles of republican government. The Eighth Amendment is a reflection of this tradition. As is commonly recognized, the Bill of Rights was drafted and ratified to assuage anti-federalist concerns that even though the Constitution clearly enumerated federal powers, it did not safeguard liberty well enough from potential abuses of these enumerated powers. The Bill of Rights was proposed by James Madison as a palliative to these concerns. In his speech in Congress wherein he proposed what would become the Bill of Rights, James Madison refers on more than one occasion to the existence of natural rights; absolute rights that check the legitimate use of federal and even state power.[31] George Mason, framer of the Virginia Declaration of Rights, on which Madison's proposal was modeled, began earlier drafts of the declaration with statements acknowledging "inherent natural Rights."[32] And Thomas Paine claimed a person possessed: "all those rights of acting as an individual for his own comfort and happiness, which are not injurious to the natural rights of others." Civil rights are positive rights secured through a social contract guaranteeing natural rights.[33]

The general acceptance of natural rights among the Framers is well documented and not highly contested, but the point demands reiteration.[34] Any reading of the Eighth Amendment must be cognizant and respectful of the fact that its origins militate it be read in reference to inherent natural rights, rights possessed of each moral agent and non-dissoluble, that is, inalienable. These rights are shorthand for the interests all mature moral agents require and are meant to restrict federal and state power insofar as there are limits to the legitimate use of force against moral agents. Thus, the Eighth Amendment is exactly what is appears to be, a restriction on the means by which the state can punish its citizenry delineated by the peoples' existence as natural rights bearers. The point of the Eighth Amendment is and always has been to emphasize a moral principle about the limits of federal power with regard to the treatment of criminals, namely, to forbid inhuman treatment such as tortuous and barbarous punishments. A ban on cruel treatment is sufficient to this end, as well as the purpose and intent of the Eighth Amendment. Justice Burger iterates this point nicely:

> From every indication, the Framers of the Eighth Amendment intended to give the phrase a meaning far different from that of its English precursor. The records of the debates in several of the state conventions called to

[31] James Madison, "Speech in Congress Proposing Constitutional Amendments," *James Madison: Writings*, comp. Jack N. Rakove (New York: Library of America, 1999), 439-440, 445, 447, 449, 452.

[32] George Mason, "The Virginia Declaration of Rights 1776," *The Papers of George Mason 1725–1792*, Vol. I 1749–1778, ed. Robert A. Rutland (Chapel Hill: University of North Carolina Press, 1970), 277, 283.

[33] Thomas Paine, *Rights of Man* in *Collected Writings* (New York: Literary Classics of the United States, 1995), 464.

[34] For a discussion on natural rights and the Framers see: Randy E. Barnett, "The Ninth Amendment: It Means What It Says," *Texas Law Review*, Vol. 85, no. 1 (Nov. 2006).

> ratify the 1789 draft Constitution submitted prior to the
> addition of the Bill of Rights show that the Framers'
> exclusive concern was the absence of any ban on tortures.
> The later inclusion of the "cruel and unusual punishments"
> clause was in response to these objections. There was no
> discussion of the interrelationship of the terms "cruel"
> and "unusual," and there is nothing in the debates
> supporting the inference that the Founding Fathers would
> have been receptive to torturous or excessively cruel
> punishments even if usual in character or authorized by
> law.[35]

Thus, along Burger's, the Framers', and the current reading, to read the Eighth Amendment as non-moral is to deviate from the original meaning of the text.

If a ban on cruel punishments is rooted in a natural, moral rights tradition, then the scope of these rights is presumed to be discernible. The Framers were Enlightenment thinkers. They believed in absolute moral values discoverable by reason. But this raises more questions than it answers. Either we accept and adopt a similar moral realist position or we do not. If we do, then we appear to be naïve moral realists and are required to demonstrate the objective moral meaning of the clause. If we do not we are left with the conclusion that the Eighth Amendment is either meaningless or merely a statement of public moral sentiment. If the latter, then it fails to restrict power since the limits of public moral sentiment are in no way restrictive, as history bears out, so as a check on power, namely the majority's over the minority's, the Eighth Amendment is meaningless. If the Eighth Amendment is meaningful it is because it is moral. So how does one determine the meaning of a moral term like cruel and apply it as law?

Cruel has been interpreted and applied many times in the past. Looking back to the decision in *Gregg v. Georgia* (1976) one is presented with a condensed history of all possible interpretations and applications. The majority's case as outlined above revolved around four basic points: the meaning of cruel, Framer intent, the law as a reflection of the will of the people, and the position of the death penalty relative to retributive and deterrence theories of punishment. Yet each of these fails to address some crucial aspect of the matter at hand.

---

[35] *Furman v. Georgia*, 408 U.S. 377 (1972) (Burger, C.J., dissenting).

With respect to the meaning of cruel, the majority declares cruel to be synonymous with excessiveness or gratuitous suffering. The historical archaeology of the concept provided above shows this to diverge from the original meaning of the term. The meaning of cruel was always barbarous, tortuous, or offensive to human dignity, not excessiveness. Of course, it is reasonable to claim that excessiveness is barbarous or offensive to human dignity such that these concepts are co-extensive. But then how is excessive to be understood? A punishment can only be excessive if it is more than is required to achieve a particular end. Thus if we are Retributivists excessive is anything over and above just desert however so defined. If we are Utilitarians excessive is the point beyond which the costs outweigh the benefits according to a calculation of the greater good. Excessiveness is, respectively, gratuitous or unnecessary. Excessiveness demands a context and in the case of punishments the context is a philosophy of punishment. Yet the Eighth Amendment is non-committal and not informative when it comes to an American philosophy of punishment. The Eighth Amendment is about means, not ends. Reading cruel as excessive demands one import into the Eighth Amendment an entire philosophy of punishment that goes well above anything in the text. Admittedly, punishment must follow a philosophy, it must have a goal. And since we are free to choose any goal we desire so long as the means fit the restrictions of the Eighth Amendment we can be Retributivists or Utilitarians. But to allow cruel to be defined by whichever theory of punishment is currently promoted allows too much flexibility since cruelty is then redefined every time we redefine our philosophy of punishment. Cruelty is supposed to function as a check, but if it is as malleable as any contingent philosophy of punishment, then it ceases to function as a check. The justices may be correct that excessiveness is determinable dependent on whatever school of punishment one adopts, but that is a far cry from proving that cruelty is exhausted by excessiveness as defined by that school of thought. Presuming the nature of barbarity is not simply about proportionate or necessary suffering we must adopt the perspective that cruelty is defined irrespective of any philosophy of punishment. All the justices have succeeded in doing is to demonstrate that the law with regard to punishment is not deductive such that moral philosophy must be applied in the adjudication of these cases.

Framer intent is a red herring. The intent of the Framers was to prevent inhuman punishments. This does nothing to clarify what "inhuman" or "cruel" means as demonstrated above, unless what is meant by Framer intent is Framer expectation. Some originalists would adjudicate Eighth Amendment cases by looking to how the Framers would have understood the clause to function. They would conclude that, since the Framers would never have anticipated or expected that the Eighth Amendment would outlaw the death penalty the death penalty cannot be a violation of it.[36] Thus, one does not simply look to the moral concept of cruelty as enshrined in the Eighth Amendment, but how that concept operated in 1791. That is, the meaning of the Eighth Amendment is exhausted by the Framers' expected application of it.

If such a reading were adopted it would threaten to make the cruel and unusual punishment clause of the Eighth Amendment antiquate— which is untenable given that it protects a natural right. But if it is not anticipated that a state legislature will propose garroting or breaking on the wheel, then since all of our current punishments were in existence during 1791 none of them can violate the Eighth Amendment; the Amendment is unnecessary. In fact, since some forms of corporal punishment did exist in 1791 we could revert to these practices.[37] But this style of interpretation misses the point; the concept of cruelty is paramount, not how the Framers expected it to be applied. The Constitutional protection of natural rights is about principles not details. These principles must be applied, and as fallible it is possible and probable that the Framers did misapply them or at the very least had a less than exhaustive understanding of all possible applications. The dialogue between Justice Antonin Scalia and Ronald Dworkin is instructive on this point.

Scalia's basic position, whether denoted "originalist" or "textualist," is that the constitution is a set of statutes and statutes rule as law by what they say. He states, "It is the *law* that governs, not the intent of the lawgiver."[38] What is law is what was promulgated. Respecting the law as

---

[36] Justice Antonin Scalia offers just such an argument below.

[37] Scalia sees this possibility and rejects it out of a "faint-hearted originalism." See: Justice Antonin Scalia, "Originalism: The Lesser Evil" in *Judges on Judging: Views from the Bench*, ed. David M. O'Brien (Washington D.C.: CQ Press, 2004), 174.

[38] Justice Antonin Scalia, "Common-Law Courts in a Civil-Law System: The Role of the United States Federal Courts in Interpreting the Constitution and Laws," in *Philosophy of Law*, 7th ed., ed. Joel Feinberg and Jules Coleman (Belmont: Wadsworth/Thomson Learning, 2004), 188.

promulgated is necessitated by the very nature and purpose of a constitution. He states:

> At an even more general theoretical level, originalism seems to me more compatible with the nature and purpose of a Constitution in a democratic system. A democratic system does not, by and large, need constitutional guarantees to insure that its laws will reflect "current values." Elections take care of that quite well. The purpose of constitutional guarantees—and in particular those constitutional guarantees of individual rights that are at the center of this controversy—is precisely to prevent the law from reflecting certain changes in original values that the society adopting the Constitution thinks fundamentally undesirable. Or, more precisely, to require the society to devote to the subject the long and hard consideration required for a constitutional amendment before those particular values can be cast aside.[39]

In response to the notion of a living constitution he maintains that the very existence of a Bill of Rights is proof against the notion that the Constitution is meant to evolve alongside current standards. A Bill of Rights is an implicit statement of distrust about evolving standards, and a protection for certain fundamental rights that do not change and cannot be lost or altered insofar as they reflect the essence of what it means to be a human being. "It certainly cannot be said that a constitution naturally suggests changeability; to the contrary, its whole purpose is to prevent change—to embed certain rights in such a manner that future generations cannot readily take them away."[40] What an interpreter must look for in the text, therefore, is the principle contained therein, not the one they wish were present. On this point Scalia and Dworkin are not so far apart. The difference between them is how they understand the principle itself. Scalia seems to maintain that principles are defined extensionally, that is, the limits of interpretation are constrained by how those who drafted a bill actually did apply it, would have applied

[39] Scalia, "Originalism: The Lesser Evil," 175.

[40] Scalia, "Common-Law Courts in a Civil-Law System: The Role of the United States Federal Courts in Interpreting the Constitution and Laws," 192.

it, or would have expected it to be applied such that the role of a justice is to merely rule as the Framers would have ruled on the case in question. In effect, Scalia seems to be looking for the Framer expectation in light of contemporary debate. Dworkin on the other hand is looking at the principle and merely asking how any reasonable person would understand it to function today so that the expectation or mindset of the Framers is no longer privileged but merely an equal voice in the debate.

In response to Scalia, Dworkin references the distinction between semantic intention and expectation intention, attributing to Scalia the former. According to Dworkin, Scalia is operating from an interpretive scheme that looks to what a Framer or lawmaker intended to say and not how they intended the law to actually be carried out. In this respect Dworkin reaffirms the distinction he often makes between a concept and a conception, namely, the notion that an idea and how the idea gets applied are distinct. In Constitutional cases this gets cashed out as the notion that the principle enshrined in a clause is not exhaustively defined by its extension as determined by the original application of the clause; rather, the principle's application expands as our understanding of it develops. Scalia, Dworkin correctly maintains, is seeking the concept inherent in the law, but as indicated above he seems to be asking how the Framers would have applied the concept today, and finds this restricted to how they actually had applied it in the past effectively privileging expectation intention over semantic intention. For example, with respect to the Eighth Amendment he refuses to accept that it could ever apply to and prohibit the use of capital punishment since not only was capital punishment a common practice in 1791 but other provisions in the Constitution acknowledge it as a legitimate punishment.[41]

Scalia correctly understands the Eighth Amendment to be a statement of abstract moral principle, namely, that cruelty is undesirable and ought not to be a part of our system of criminal punishment. But he states that the definition of this principle is easily at hand and that what is meant by cruel is what society and the Framers held to be cruel when the Eighth Amendment was ratified in 1791, that is, its extensional definition. So if we want to know what cruel means we simply have to see what the Framers thought was cruel. Although this may be difficult, one thing is certain; they did not find capital punishment to be cruel since they made accommodations for it in other places in the Constitution. This is true, but not conclusive and probably irrelevant. What one is seeking in

---

[41] Cf. Scalia, "Originalism: The Lesser Evil," 175.

interpreting a moral clause is not an understanding of how the Framers would have applied it but how the concept applies today. Past applications are not definitive in determining the exhaustive meaning of a moral clause; previous interpreters could have erred, as the Supreme Court recognizes every time it overturns itself.

The Eighth Amendment expresses the moral principle that human beings ought not to be treated cruelly. This is different than maintaining that the Eighth Amendment means that the Framers found punishments X, Y, and Z to be cruel, but A, B, and C not. The concept is the principle and the conception is the contingent application of the principle.[42] The former ought to take priority since the latter is predicated on it. Scalia's position is difficult to grasp because he vacillates between which to prioritize. If cruelty is to be avoided, then it ought to be avoided in all cases even if some of these cases had previously been deemed acceptable. Cruelty cannot be defined by Framer intent other than with reference to the less than helpful notion that their intent was to secure human dignity consistent with their natural rights heritage.

The idea that the meaning of cruel is determined by a consensus of the people or their representatives in the legislature is contrary to the purpose of the Bill of Rights. The Bill of Rights was adopted to guarantee fundamental rights restricting governmental power. It is for the protection of the minority against the majority. With respect to the meaning of the term cruel itself, if a moral realist position is adopted then neither the meaning of this term nor its extension changes regardless of the will of the people. Contrary to Chief Justice Warren regarding the "evolving standards of decency" it must be maintained that the meaning of cruel does not evolve even if society's standards do. Rather, moral progress is marked by a clearer understanding of the objectively determinable term "cruel." Perhaps such a notion is what is intimated by Justice Marshall's claim that a fully informed populace would reject the death penalty, if by fully informed he meant not merely factually informed but morally cultivated.[43] Such a position is in direct opposition to Justice Burger who claims that the application of the cruel and unusual punishments clause

---

[42] Cf. Ronald Dworkin, *Taking Rights Seriously* (Cambridge: Harvard University Press, 1978), Chap. 5.

[43] See *Furman V. Georgia* 408 U.S. 238 (Marshall, J. concurring) This claim may be contentious, but it is worth considering moral knowledge as a form of relevant knowledge.

must change as do society's mores.[44] But cruelty is not a relative concept, at least not if it is a protection of inherent, natural, moral rights.

Finally, the argument that the death penalty is consistent with both retributive and deterrent theories of punishment is true, but trivially so. The Eighth Amendment is about the restriction of means of punishment, not a declaration of the ends or goals of the American penal system. It may be true that both retributive and deterrent ends are achieved through the death penalty, but that does not mean that it is not a barbaric means of accomplishing these ends and so a cruel punishment. The claim to excessiveness is often addressed in these regards to either demonstrate that death is not excessive and so not cruel because it serves a deterrent or retributive end or that it is excessive because it does not do so. But as noted above, even if relevant these arguments are far from conclusive. The notion of excessiveness is a problematic definition of cruelty and a correct interpretation is non-committal regarding the ends of punishment. Torture can be justified through retributive and deterrent arguments, but it is always cruel and acknowledged as such by those who would allow for the death penalty on the same retributive or deterrence theory. What is required is a definition of cruelty that allows for a more precise meaning of a moral term which is reflective of the concern for inherent human dignity as reflected in the natural rights tradition of the Framers.

One could argue, as Scalia appears to, that the clause prohibiting cruel and unusual punishments could be given meaning by an extensional definition, that is, with reference to those instances contained under the concept such that to know what is cruel is to merely enumerate those instances of punishment the Framers understood to be cruel, e.g. breaking on the wheel, garroting, the rack, thumbscrews, etc. Such a procedure would effectively be to interpret the clause not with respect to Framers' intent, that is, we know they intended to prohibit inhuman and barbarous punishments, but to delineate which punishments qualify as barbarous with reference to how the Framers would have expected the clause to function. As promising as this may seem it is impracticable insofar as it demands not only clairvoyance, but it also relegates the Eighth Amendment to a vestigial characteristic of the Constitution. Nobody envisions a regression in our disciplinary practices such that we would actually propose a punishment the Framers opposed, such as garroting. But there is a further problem.

---

[44] Ibid., (Burger, J. dissenting).

The crimes condemned by the Eighth Amendment were condemned because they were cruel. The concept "cruel" meant inhuman, barbarous, and tortuous just as it does today. The concept was not defined by specific instances; rather the concept is what was used to pick out these instances. The Framers perceived cruel behavior as behavior that was demeaning and dehumanizing. They maintained that this type of behavior was unacceptable and the government must be prevented from exacting this type of punishment on its citizens. They did not need a laundry list of punishments in order to come to the concept, nor did they have an exhaustive understanding of all possible punishments that could fall under the concept. To paraphrase James Iredell: let anyone make what collection or enumeration of cruel punishments he pleases, I will immediately mention twenty or thirty more.[45] An enumeration of cruel punishments is only as limited as our imaginations. It is not the list that is instructive, but the concept used to enumerate instances.

One could, if one were so inclined, ask what all the particular punishments that the Framers condemned shared and thus through a conceptual archaeology unearth the concept of cruelty used by the Framers thus remaining true to some original meaning. But this will merely push the problem back a level since any concept utilized by the Framers would reduce ultimately to something like, "all these instances are cruel insofar as they are an affront to human dignity." The concept they would be applying, in the above example "human dignity," would be a moral concept leading back to the original problem, namely, giving legal precision to a moral notion.

Cruelty needs to be made more precise with moral language and through moral argument. It cannot be done through a laundry list of actual or expected instances of cruel punishments. In order to fill it out we will invariably turn to other moral concepts such as dignity or humane treatment. All of these concepts will then likewise have to be filled out through their application and this can only be done through the use of judgment. Yet reliance on the discretion of the Justices of the Supreme Court in the determination of vague moral terms is often, and rightly, seen to be quite problematic. The debate over the meaning of "obscene" is difficult enough,[46] let alone the determination of cruelty. And there is the legitimate

[45] Paraphrase of James Iredell in "Debates in the Convention of the State of North Carolina, on the Adoption of the Federal Constitution (July 29, 1788)" in 4 *The Debates in the Several State Conventions on the Adoption of the Federal Constitution* 1, 167 (Jonathan Elliot ed., 2nd ed. 1907). Iredell's original statement was with regard to the enumeration of individual natural rights.

[46] See: *Miller v. California* 413 U.S. 15 (1973).

concern that one's natural rights should not be left to the discretion of five judges. But in moral matters judgment is our only guide. Thus we would be wise to adopt the position of Madison. "I go on this great republican principle, that the people will have virtue and intelligence to select men of virtue and wisdom. Is there no virtue among us? If there be not, we are in a wretched situation. No theoretical checks—no form of government can render us secure."[47] One must, perhaps naively, premise the strength of republican government on not merely checks and balances but also a hope and faith in virtue and reflection. With respect to the use of judicial discretion in the application of the law, Justice Brennan provides the quintessential case in point.

III. JUSTICE BRENNAN AND A MORAL READING OF THE EIGHTH AMENDMENT

Justice Brennan argues that the death penalty is always an affront to human dignity so it is always cruel. He bases his position on a moral interpretation of "cruel" wherein it means offensive to human dignity. Thus, his case is predicated on adjudicating what is and is not an affront to dignity. Some perceive this moral reading of the text to be beyond the scope of judicial discretion; the act of activist judges who can through their own idiosyncratic moral positions justify any ruling they see fit. But for Justice Brennan his reading is not an unfounded interpretation of the text, but a faithful reading of the principle enshrined therein; the role of a judge is to interpret and apply the law, and as morally grounded moral philosophy is one tool in this process.

Brennan's jurisprudence explains fully his position regarding the Eighth Amendment. For Brennan, the law is not merely about statutes and precedents, but principles and values all of which are rooted firmly in a natural law tradition.[48] In this regard, he is more a kindred spirit of the Framers than those that would offer a formal or literal reading of the texts. The Bill of Rights is a protection of natural rights; rights possessed of all human beings insofar as they are human and thus have certain fundamental interests. Judicial review is the process by which law is

---

[47] James Madison, "Speech in the Virginia Ratifying Convention on Judicial Power," *James Madison: Writings,* comp. Jack N. Rakove (New York: Library of America, 1999), 398.

[48] Cf. Justice William J. Brennan Jr., *An Affair with Freedom: A Collection of His Opinions and Speeches Drawn from his First Decade as a United States Supreme Court Justice,* ed. Stephen J. Friedman (New York: Antheneum, 1967), 320-2 passim.

judged to either be in accord with or a violation of these natural rights. If the law is adjudicated to violate these rights, then it is deemed a violation of inherent moral rights, that is, the law is an illegitimate infringement of fundamental interests; it is adjudicated immoral and it is thereby invalidated. This process is consistent with and demanded by the natural rights tradition from which the Constitution and Bill of Rights derive. The Eighth Amendment is part of this tradition. Brennan maintains that it is the obligation of a justice in constitutional cases to interpret the law in light of the principles and values in it to resolve contemporary debates.[49] The Constitution, specifically the Bill of Rights, is a statement of principles and values predicated on inherent human rights and dignity—a position espoused likewise by George Mason and James Madison—and must be interpreted as such if it is to remain effective and relevant to contemporary debates; debates grounded in the very values and principles on which the document rests.

With respect to the Eighth Amendment, it is paramount to present concern to understand that Brennan understood the Bill of Rights, and specifically the Eighth Amendment, as a check on majority rule and a statement about the relation between the individual and the state. He states: "Faith in democracy is one thing, blind faith quite another. Those who drafted our Constitution understood the difference. One cannot read the text without admitting that it embodies substantive value choices; it places certain values beyond the power of any legislature."[50] One of these values is human dignity; a value that denies any state authority the power to dehumanize a person. He continues:

> As I have said in my opinions, I view the Eighth Amendment's prohibition on cruel and unusual punishments as embodying to a unique degree moral principles that substantively restrain the punishments our civilized society may impose on those persons who transgress its laws. Foremost among the moral principles recognized in our cases and inherent in the prohibition is the primary principle that the state, even as it punishes, must treat its citizens in a manner consistent with their

[49] Cf. Justice William J. Brennan Jr., "The Constitution of the United States: Contemporary Ratification," in *Judges on Judging: Views from the Bench,* ed. David M. O'Brien (Washington, D.C.: CQ Press, 2004), 184.

[50] Ibid., 186.

intrinsic worth as human beings. A punishment must not be so severe as to be utterly and irreversibly degrading to the very essence of human dignity. Death for whatever crime and under all circumstances is a truly awesome punishment. The calculated killing of a human being by the state involves, by its very nature, an absolute denial of the executed person's humanity. The most vile murder does not, in my view, release the state from constitutional restraints on the destruction of human dignity. Yet an executed person has lost the very right to have rights, now or ever. For me, then, the fatal constitutional infirmity of capital punishment is that it treats members of the human race as non-humans, as objects to be toyed with and discarded. It is, indeed, "cruel and unusual." It is thus inconsistent with the fundamental premise of the Clause that even the most base criminal remains a human being possessed of some potential, at least, for common human dignity.[51]

The Eighth Amendment restricts the means of punishment to only those punishments that are not an affront to the inherent dignity of each human being. Cruel is defined with reference to what type of things human beings are. If human beings are natural rights bearers possessed of inherent human dignity, then cruel treatment, insofar as it is inhumane treatment, is whatever disparages human dignity. It is beyond the government to remove from such a being her inalienable and absolute moral worth, regardless of how heinous her crime. The death penalty is the most severe of all possible punishments because it denies of a human being, as Brennan notes above, their right to have rights, their potential for common human dignity, that is, their very status as a human being.[52] As Benjamin Rush noted in the opening quote of this article, the death penalty treats people as property, as disposable, or, as Brennan reinforces, as things to be toyed with and discarded.[53]

Implicit in a notion of human dignity, of humane treatment is that each human being must be treated as an irreplaceable and valuable

---

[51] Ibid., 192.

[52] Ibid.

[53] Ibid.

being capable of moral rejuvenation even if past transgressions militate against such an assessment. Roger Sherman of Connecticut in opposition to a bill proposing the death penalty for forgery remarked, "he had known persons who had been convicted of this crime, that had afterwards reformed."[54] Death is unfit for those who still possess the capacity for reform, since this capacity is part and parcel of what it is to be a moral agent. Death is only fitting for those who are disposable, those who lack the capacity for moral change. But this type of assessment or knowledge is beyond human understanding. Perhaps the check the Eighth Amendment demands is one against moral arrogance, the attitude that it is possible to condemn an entire person or an entire life. Human dignity demands humility in judgment. To take another's life is to make an unwarranted judgment about them, and irreparably so.[55]

Brennan's position, as well as others who would make the constitutionally based abolitionist argument, is based on a particular conception of the human being. Each person, in order to be treated as a moral agent, must be treated as capable of reform. With respect to which philosophy of punishment is most appropriate for the United States, the Eighth Amendment only places restrictions on the means applied, not the ends chosen. Death, however, is never a fitting means.

Allowing moral argumentation and philosophy into the judicial process will unsettle many, but insofar as the Constitution does contain moral clauses any form of adjudication is going to demand moral argumentation. It is up to the justices to determine the meaning of these clauses even if they conflict with how the Framers themselves understood them. If one is looking for abstract moral principles, then one is only beholden to the demands of reason and compelled only by the best argument.

---

[54] *U.S. House Journal.* 1790. 1st Cong., 2nd Sess., 6 Apr. 1573-4.

[55] For discussion of this point see: Jeffrie G. Murphy, *Getting Even: Forgiveness and Its Limits* (New York: Oxford University Press, 2003) Chap. 8.

ETHICS AND ITS CONTROVERSIAL ASSUMPTIONS
Tibor R. Machan

Whether ethics even exists is often in dispute. That is to say, whether claims such as "People should be honest" or "Children should be cared for" or, again, "Treating members of racial groups with prejudice is wrong" can ever be true is widely disputed. Many believe ethical claims like these and claims such as those made in the various sciences are radically different because claims in the sciences are subject to certain kinds of demonstration which are not available when we attempt to show ethical claims to be true. Another source of serious skepticism about ethics comes from the fact that a good many natural and social scientists think that people cannot be morally blamed for what they do; instead their conduct is explainable by various causes and the agent's initiative, will, or choice is but an illusion.

Ordinary folks, too, are at times convinced that people act badly only because something made them do so, some event in their upbringing, some biological component of their makeup, or some factor of the culture to which they belong. (We tend to *explain* our own bad conduct more readily but *blame* other people for theirs! And, conversely, we tend to take *credit* for our good conduct but often dismiss that of others as having been the *result* of various impersonal factors.)

So whether ethics is a *bona fide* part of human life is not self-evident, nor obvious. In order for there to be ethics, some other facts must already obtain. Such claims as "Judy should not lie," or "The president of the United Sates of America ought to be honest with the citizenry" assume that Judy and the president have a choice about what they will do. As Immanuel Kant believed, "ought" implies "can." This means that if one *ought to do* something, it must be that one *can either do or not do it*. It also assumes that Judy, the president and anyone who would look into the matter can identify certain standards of conduct to be used in figuring out what we should or should not do.

Some claim that Kant's insight is wrong and that we need not be free in the sense of having the capacity either to do or not to do something, as a matter of our own initiative or choice, all things being equal, because this would violate the laws of causality which make it impossible for two different outcomes to result from identical circumstances.[1] Nevertheless, these philosophers hold to what is called a compatibilist position such that people are still responsible for their actions, even though they couldn't have acted some other way than they actually did. By "responsible" they mean, however, not that they could have done something else under the same circumstances but that they were, in fact, instrumental in what came about—they played a causal role in a sequence of causes that resulted in what we are evaluating about them.

Such a view, however, is arguably not what amounts to a genuine, *bona fide* moral perspective. Both ordinary morality and law take it that human beings are generally free to take different actions from identical circumstances, otherwise the idea that they ought to have done otherwise—for example, not kidnapped or assaulted someone, not cheated on their wives, not murdered millions during the Holocaust—could not apply. Arguably, then the compatibilist position is a sort of attempt to eat one's cake and have it, also—being true to determinism but also to the requirements of the moral point of view.

In this discussion I will take it that either ethics is a genuine part of human life, in which case people are normally free to choose between alternative courses of conduct all else being equal, or there is no morality and it is all a matter of what will be will be—*que sera, sera.*

First, then, for ethics to be real, it must be that we can exercise some genuine choices, that we have the capacity to initiate some actions. If this were impossible, the idea that we should (or should not) act in such and such a fashion would have no application in human life. Second, ethics requires that some principles that apply to conduct be identifiable or objective. Unless we all can learn those very general principles, ethics has no place in our lives. It consists, after all, of such principles of conduct that pertain to all human beings. Moral or ethical principles pertain to action, how we should conduct ourselves, on what basis we should choose or select what we will do. To succeed at living a human life which is morally good, some principles would have to be followed. "Morally good" here means: being excellent as a human being in one's life but as a matter of choice, of one's own initiative, not accidentally. So being tall or talented or beautiful are not aspects of moral

---

[1] See John Kekes, "'Ought Implies Can' and Kinds of Morality," *Philosophical Quarterly*, Vol. 34 (1984), 460-467. See, also, his *Facing Evil* (Princeton: Princeton University Press, 1991), which includes the bulk of the discussion from the aforementioned paper as well as others, such as "Freedom," *Pacific Philosophical Quarterly*, Vol. 61 (1980), 368-385.

excellence, whereas being honest, courageous and prudent would be, if ethics is indeed a *bona fide* dimension of human living.

If we could not exercise genuine choices, morality would be impossible since no one could help what he or she is doing. It would all be a matter of good and bad things simply happening, as indeed they often do at the hands of nature, as it were: when tornadoes or earthquakes or diseases strike. *Que sera, sera*, period.

If we could not identify moral principles, we could never make a sensible selection from among alternative courses of conduct. Depending on what we aim for, we can identify the principles that will enable us to reach our goal. This is clearly evident in such fields as medicine, engineering and business. Thus, it seems that this second requirement of ethics, that we can identify principles of conduct, might be satisfied. But we will need to explore that further to be able to tell.

Let me explore briefly whether these two assumptions are reasonable or merely prejudice or myth as some folks believe, ones who would consign ethics to the dustbin of pre-science, akin to demonology or witchcraft. The answers I will reach cannot be considered conclusive—there isn't enough time and space to carry out a full investigation. But we will have a chance to look at the major points for and against the assumptions. Without some idea about whether they are true, ethics itself is left unsupported—it could just as easily be in the class of the occult, such as astrology or palmistry.

I. FREE WILL?

The first matter to address is whether we have free will—not necessarily all of us, all of the time but, rather, we as a rule, normally. In other words, are human beings, as they have appeared throughout history in their innumerable diverse circumstances (though not when incapacitated or significantly damaged or as bare infants) capable of bringing about, of their own initiative, the behavior in which they engage?

1.1. Against Free Will—Nature's Laws versus Free Will

First, one of the major objections against free will is that nature is governed by a set of laws, mainly the laws of physics. The argument here is that all material substances are controlled by these laws and we human beings are basically complicated versions of material substances. Therefore, whatever governs material substance in the universe must also govern human life.

Social science, for one, which studies human beings in their social relations, looks into some of the causes that produce our behavior. So does neuroscience, a sub-discipline of biology, in its study of our individual brains-minds. In each case what is studied are the causes of behavior. So, the only difference between the rest of nature and ourselves, as far as these branches of science are concerned, is that we are more complicated, not that we are not governed by the same principles or laws of nature.

Most definitely, it is argued, no such thing as an original cause is evident in the rest of nature, something that would have to be possible for free will to exist. As one advocate of determinism puts it, "[T]he best response to the demand for an explanation of the relation between an originator and decisions is that an explanation cannot be given. We have to regard this relation as primitive or unanalyzable."[2] In other words, originating or initiating some action seems nothing more than a myth or an unexplainable fact, for which no evidence or argument can be given.

The determinist claims that all our actions, including decisions, are more sensibly taken to be effects of some prior events. It is the determinist's view that everything we do is the effect of some set of causal circumstances. This makes better sense, say the determinists, than leaving things unexplained, mysterious.

1.2. Affirming Initiative

Now, in response one might argue that nature exhibits innumerable different domains, distinct not only in their complexity but also in the kinds of beings they include. There are, to be sure, many domains where we find the familiar cause and effect situation clearly evident—for example, on the billiard table, in geological movements, and in the motion of the planets. But there are areas where something else appears to be going on. For example, is the cause of a musical composition, the composer, itself some effect of a prior cause, so that the composer makes no original contribution?[3]

So, "causal" reasoning does not necessarily rule out that there might be something in nature that exhibits agent or original causation, the phenom-

---

[2] Ted Honderich, *How Free Are You? The Determinism Problem* (Oxford: Oxford University Press, 1993), 42-3.

[3] Even in physical reality, as in the freezing of water, the causal relationship isn't exactly what it is in other domains. The freezing occurs by way of what has been called "downward causation," instead of the more familiar "action-reaction" causation. For more on this point, see Robert Laughlin, *A Different University* (New York: Basic Books, 2005).

enon whereby a thing causes some of its own behavior. Causal interactions depend on the nature of the beings that interact, what they are. So one cannot rule out, *a priori* (before investigation), that some beings could have the capacity to act on their own initiative.

Thus it seems that there might be in nature a form of existence that exhibits free will. Whether there is or is not is something to be discovered, not ruled out by a narrow worldview or metaphysics that restricts everything to being just one kind of thing so that everything has just one kind of causal characteristics. Nature appears to be composed of many types and kinds of things and thus does not have to exclude free will.

So, free will seems to be possible, even in a world of causality. Whether free will actually exists we'll examine shortly.

1.3. We Cannot Know of Free Will

Now, another reason why some think that free will is not possible is that the dominant mode of studying, inspecting or examining nature is what we call "empiricism." In other words, many believe that the only way we know about nature is by observing it with our various sensory organs. But since the sensory organs do not give us direct evidence of such a thing as free will, there really isn't any such thing. Since no observable evidence for free will exists, therefore free will does not exist.

1.4. We Can Know Free Will

But the doctrine that empiricism captures all forms of knowing is wrong—we know many things not simply through observation but through a combination of observation, inferences, and theory construction. (Consider, even the purported knowledge that empiricism is our form of knowledge is not "known" empirically!)

For one, many features of the universe, including criminal guilt, are detected without eyewitnesses but by way of theories which serve the purpose of best explaining what we do have before us to observe. This is true, also, even in the natural sciences. Many of the complex phenomena or facts in biology, astrophysics, subatomic physics, botany, chemistry— not to mention psychology—consist not of what we see or detect by observation but are inferred by way of a theory. The theory that explains things best—most completely and most consistently—is the best answer to the question as to what is going on.

Free will may well turn out to be in this category. In other words, free will may not be something that we can see directly, but what best explains what we do see in human life. This may include, for example, the many mistakes that human beings make in contrast to the few mistakes that other animals make. We also notice that human beings do all kinds of odd things that cannot be accounted for in terms of mechanical causation, the type associated with physics. We can examine a person's background and find that some people with bad childhoods turn out to be decent, while others become crooks. Free will, then, amounts to a very helpful explanation. For now all we need to consider is that this may well be so, and if empiricism does not allow for it, so much the worse for empiricism. One could know something because it explains something else better than any alternative. And that is not strict empirical knowledge.

1.5. Free Will Is Weird

Another matter that very often counts against free will is that the rest of (even living) beings in nature do not exhibit it. Dogs, cats, lizards, fish, frogs, etc., have no free will and therefore it appears arbitrary to impute it to human beings. Why should we be free to do things when the rest of nature lacks any such capacity? It would be an impossible aberration. Some opponents of the free will idea, such as the behaviorist psychologist B. F. Skinner, have stressed this objection.[4]

1.6. Free Will is Natural

The answer here is similar to what I gave earlier. To wit, there is enough variety in nature—some things swim, some fly, some just lie there, some breathe, some grow, while others do not; so there is plenty of evidence of plurality of types and kinds of things in nature. Discovering that something has free will could be yet another addition to all the varieties of nature. Determinism seems to depend upon adherence to a very specific ontology, in terms of which everything must be a given kind of thing, one that can only move when prompted by something else, and this is not something that can be shown to hold universally so as to preclude free will.

1.7. God Doesn't Allow Free

Will. There is also the theological argument to the effect that if God knows everything, he/she knows the future, so what we do is unalterable. If someone knows that some future event will occur, e.g., that Haley's Comet will come nearest to earth at some given time in the future, then whatever is involved in that event cannot have a choice about it. So if God knows that you will have three children, then you have no genuine choice about that matter. It has to turn out that way.

---

[4] B. F. Skinner, *Beyond Freedom and Dignity* (Garden City: Bantam Books, 1972).

1.8. God's "knowledge" is Mysterious

But God's knowledge is not likely to be the kind human beings have, indeed, just what it is is a mystery. So nothing much can be inferred from it. It is mistake to confuse what would follow from a human being's knowing the future versus God's "knowledge" of the future. The latter is entirely different from the former and so the implications wouldn't be the same either.

1.9. For Free Will

Let's now consider whether free will actually does exist. I'll offer four arguments in support of an affirmative answer. (They are not uniquely my arguments but ones that have been proposed throughout the philosophical community.) Thus far we have only considered whether free will is possible. But does it exist? The following points support that contention.

1.10. Are We Determined to be Determinists—or not?

If we are fully determined by impersonal forces to behave as we do, this implies that what we think is also so determined. And then the belief that determinism is true is also a result of such forces, not something we come to learn as a matter of choosing to use our minds well. But the same holds for the belief that determinism is false. There is nothing one can do about whatever one believes—one was determined to believe it.

1.11. Doesn't Judgment Require independence?

If, however, there is no way to take an independent stance and consider the arguments in an unprejudiced manner, because all the various forces making us assimilate the evidence either cause us to believe or disbelieve in determinism, then both the belief in and the rejection of determinism are a matter of such forces and an independent assessment of the topic is possible. One either turns out to be a determinist or not and in neither case can we appraise the issue objectively because we are predetermined to have a view on the matter one way or the other, ad infinitum.

And then, paradoxically, we'll never be able to resolve this debate, since there is no way of obtaining an objective, unbiased assessment—we aren't free to judge such matters. Indeed, the very idea of philosophical, scientific or judicial objectivity, as well as of ever coming to know anything, has to do with being free. Thus, if we're engaged in this enterprise of learning about truth and distinguishing it from falsehood, we are committed to the idea that human beings have some measure of mental freedom. This view was put forward by Immanuel Kant, the eighteenth century German philosopher, as well as by Nathaniel Branden, a psychologist who defends free will.[5]

---

[5] Nathaniel Branden, *The Psychology of Self-Esteem* (Garden City: Bantam Books, 1969).

1.12. We Should All Become Determinists

Everyone who accepts determinism would also have all those who reject it accept the view, as well. This is especially true of those involved in the argument about the topic. Both those who embrace free will and those who embrace determinism hold that the others ought to change their minds and join them in holding their position. Of course, if it is right, that is what we all should believe.

1.13. The Dilemma of Determinism

However, there's a dilemma afoot in determinists imploring others to accept their views, to change their minds. Since the determinist holds we cannot help what we believe—such matters aren't up to us, there is no choice about the matter—the determinist has no basis to ask us to believe in determinism, to ask that we ought to do so rather than believe in "the illusion of free will." As Kant also said, "ought" implies "can." That is, if one ought to believe in or do something, this implies that one has a free choice in the matter; it implies that it is up to us whether we will hold determinism or free will as the better doctrine. That, in turn, assumes that we are free.

So, even arguing for determinism assumes that we are not determined to believe in free will but that it is a matter of our making certain choices about arguments, evidence, and thinking itself. We run across this paradox when we find people who blame us for not accepting the view that people's fate is not in their hands so we should not blame them. Blaming some while denying that anyone should be blamed is a paradox, one which troubles a deterministic position. In one book defending determinism, the author ends by posing the following question: "If ['Left Wing politics is less given to attitudes and policies which have something of the assumption of Free Will in them'], should one part of the response . . . be a move to the Left in politics? I leave you with that bracing question."[6] Yet can this be a genuine question, if the answer is predetermined and one either will or will not move Left or Right and has no choice in the matter?[7]

This line of attack on determinism suggests that free will exists for human beings as a matter of necessity or necessarily, since any

---

[6] Op. cit., Honderich, 129.

[7] It cannot, as argued by Joseph M. Boyle, G. Grisez and O. Tollefsen, *Free Choice* (Notre Dame: University of Notre Dame Press, 1976). See, also, James N. Jordan, "Determinism's Dilemma," *Review of Metaphysics 23* (Sept. 1969), 48-66. My own *Initiative—Human Agency and Society* (Stanford: Hoover Institution Press, 2000), makes these points.

belief one might have about anything, including whether this matter can be rationally resolved, presupposes the ability of the human mind to address the issue without impediments that would distort how it is with the topic.

1.14. Free Will Is A Self-Delusion

Many prominent thinkers hold that free will doesn't exist but we need to believe in it. The famous astrophysicist Stephen Hawking, for example, holds this position, as did even B. F. Skinner. Some even argue that the belief in free will, albeit wrong, is produced in us by evolutionary forces. Such a false belief has survival value. (Some hold the same view about religion, that the uniquely religious content of religious beliefs is false but has survival value for us.)

1.15. We Often Know We Are Free

Aside from what has already been said here about the basis of free will, it may also be noted that since in many contexts of our lives introspective knowledge is taken very seriously, such knowledge about free will needs also to be taken seriously. When one goes to a doctor and is asked, "Are you in pain?" and one answers, "Yes," and the doctor says "Where is the pain?" and you say, "It's in my knee," the doctor doesn't say, "Why, you can't know, this is not public evidence; I will now get verifiable, direct evidence of where you hurt." In fact the patient's evidence is very good if not the best evidence. Witnesses at trials give such evidence as they report about what they have seen, relying as they do on their memory, something they access introspectively. That is the source of the confidence we have in claims such as "This indeed is what I have seen or heard." It involves reference to something we recall from memory and is thus something within us, not evident to others without our testimony or report. Even in the various sciences people report on what they've read on surveys or seen on gauges or instruments or studies. Thus they are giving us introspective evidence.

Introspection is one source of evidence that we take as reasonably reliable. So what should we make of the fact that a lot of people do believe and say things like, "Damn it, I didn't make the right choice," or "I neglected to do something." They report to us, furthermore, that they have made various choices, decisions, etc., or that they intended this or that but not another thing. They, furthermore, often blame themselves for not having done something, thus implying that they know that they made a choice (for which they are taking responsibility).

In short, there is abundant evidence from people all around us of their experience of the existence of their own free choices. This cannot just be ruled out, since it would also undercut much else we take very seriously, indeed treat as decisive, coming from such sources.

1.16. But Science Shows that there is no Free Will

It is often held that scientists have shown that free will does not exist. How? By having unearthed, in numerous cases, causal factors that explain what we do—our thinking and our behavior. Psychology, physiology, economics and numerous other fields of science aim to show why people behave as they do, how come they hold various views and act as they do. So, it is clear, then, that no such thing as free will exists.

1.17. Science Discovers Free Will

Arguably, however, what scientists and those who claim that they have shown there is no free will actually have done is ruled out free will by virtue of certain assumptions they hold about the world. The most widely held assumption is that every event must have a cause, and only events can be causes. (We have already touched on this above.) For example, B. F. Skinner does not actually prove that all our behavior is traceable to prior events. Instead, he holds to a certain metaphysical position that implies this.[8]

Moreover, there is also the evidence from the field of psychophysics that we do have the capacity for self-monitoring and self-determination. According to some of the scientists in this discipline, the human brain has the kind of structure that allows us, so to speak, to govern ourselves. We can inspect our lives, we can detect where we're going, and we can, therefore, change course. The human brain itself makes all this possible. The brain, because of its structure, can monitor itself—that is, its higher regions can influence the rest—and as a result we can decide whether to continue in a certain pattern or to change that pattern and go in a different direction. This is how we change habits, restrain impulses, control our temper, "watch what we eat," alter our developed motor skills in, say, how we play the piano, or even change our established opinions. That is the sort of free will that is demonstrable.

For example Roger W. Sperry maintains that there's evidence for free will in this sense.[9] This view depends on a number of points I have already mentioned. It assumes, for example, that there can be different kinds of

---

[8] See, for more, Tibor R. Machan, *The Pseudo Science of B. F. Skinner* (New Rochelle: Arlington House Publishing Co., Inc., 1974).

[9] Roger W. Sperry, *Science and Moral Priority* (New York: Columbia University Press, 1983).

causes in nature and, also, that the functioning of the brain as a complex neuropsychological system could manifest self-causation. An organism with our kind of brain could cause some mental functions to occur via what Sperry calls a process of "downward causation." (Sperry argues that there is some evidence of such causation even apart from how the human organism's higher mental activities occur, for example, in the way water freezes.)

Now the sort of thing Sperry thinks possible is evident in our lives. We make plans and then, upon reconsideration (which at times takes but a fraction of a second) revise them. We explore alternatives and decide to follow one of these. We change a course of conduct we have embarked upon, or continue with it. And most revealingly, we resist temptations, act despite the desire to do something else, and gradually build up good habits which, at first, were difficult to cultivate. In other words, there is a locus of individual self-responsibility or initiative—or, to use Ted Honderich's term, "origination"—that is evident in the way in which we look upon ourselves, and the way in which we in fact behave.

1.18. Some Cautionary Points

There clearly are cases of conduct in which some persons behave as they do because they were determined to do so by certain identifiable forces beyond their control. A brain tumor, a severe childhood trauma or some other intrusive force sometimes incapacitates people. This is evident in those occasional cases when a person who engaged in criminal behavior is shown to have had no control over what he or she did. Someone who actually had no capacity to control his or her behavior, could not control his or her own thinking or judgment and was, thus, moved by something other than his own will, cannot be said to possess a *bona fide* free will.

1.19. Compatibilism

Those who deny that we have free will would seem to be unable to make sense of our distinction between cases in which one controls one's behavior and those in which one is being moved by forces over which he or she has no control. When we face the latter sort of case, we still admit that the behavior could be good or bad but we deny that it is morally and legally significant—it is more along lines of acts of nature or God by being out of the agent's control. This is also why philosophers who discuss ethics but deny free will have trouble distinguishing between morality and value theory—e.g., some utilitarians, Marxists. Morality concerns how we ought to act (or the rightness of conduct), whereas value theory deals with what is good and bad and why. It is possible to address the latter field without taking a side on the free will issue. But that is not so with the former.

Some, as we have already mentioned, will defend the view that even if we have no *ultimate* control over our actions—even if our behavior, the judgments which we make, or our character is controlled by forces such as the environment or our genetic make-up—we may still speak of ethics or morality. These compatibilists, however, mean by the term "ethics" or "morality" something different from what the terms would mean if we did possess free will.

For compatibilists ethics concerns the standards of good behavior, in conformity with rightness regardless of how it came about that one conformed or did not conform to those standards. Ethics, along these lines, concerns values and how to secure them, without implying that one could, of one's own initiative, exert control over whether these values would be achieved. Accordingly, then, without personal responsibility or agency—where one is the cause of what one does, whereby one initiates or originates one's significant actions—ethics would amount to something drastically different from what we usually mean by the term.

Given the way compatibilists see human action—namely, that it is possible to have both a causal explanation of it as well as the agent being responsible for the conduct—the theory appears to succeed better than all others, including the one dubbed agent causal free will. In fact, however, the compatibilist doctrine does not allow for personal *moral* responsibility, however much its proponents so insist. No *bona fide*, ultimate personal responsibility can be attached to behavior that is, so to speak, softly determined. If one's character has been molded so that one will have integrity and be honest, generous, and so forth, and when one exhibits integrity and is indeed honest, generous and so forth, one cannot reasonably be said to be responsible for any of this. It is whatever molded one's character that would have produced and explained one's honesty, generosity and so forth. Any kind of moral credit would be unwarranted and amount to an illusion, not something well deserved. (It is indeed for this reason that John Rawls, the most prominent political philosopher of the twentieth century, denied that there is any morally significant difference between those who produce wealth and those who do not—as he put it in his most important work, "The assertion that a man deserves the superior character that enables him to make the effort to cultivate his abilities is . . . problematic; for his character depends in large part upon fortunate family and social circumstances for which he can claim no credit."[10] The very foundation of the welfare state rests, as Rawls saw it, on denying that differences in effort are of any moral significance. Of course, Rawls like many others did paradoxically urge that we all recognize this and if one does not, one is *morally remiss*!)

Compatibilism, then, is a dead end and no significant, *bona fide* moral (as distinct from value) theory can rest on it. Furthermore, there is a direct impact on politics from the denial of *bona fide* free will—it implies moral and legal egalitarianism, just as had been claimed by the famous American defense attorney Clarence Darrow.

1.20. Is Free Will Well Founded?

So these several reasons provide a kind of argumentative collage in support of the free will position. Can anyone do better with this issue? I don't know. I think it's best to ask only for what is the best of the various competing theories. Are human beings doing what they do solely as the consequences of forces acting on them? Or do they have the capacity to take charge of their lives, often neglect to do so properly or effectively, make stupid choices? Which supposition best explains the human world and its complexities around us?

I think the free will view makes much better sense. It explains, much better than do deterministic theories, how it is possible that human life involves such an array of possibilities, accomplishments as well as defeats, joys as well as sorrows, creation as well as destruction. It explains, also, why in human life there is so much change—in language, custom, style, art, and science. Unlike other living beings, for which what is possible is pretty much fixed by instincts and reflexes—even if some extraordinary behavior may be elicited, by way of extensive prodding in laboratories or, at times, in the face of unusual natural developments—people initiate much of what they do, for better and for worse. From their most distinctive capacity of forming ideas and theories, to those of artistic and athletic inventiveness, human beings remake the world without, so to speak, having to do so! This, moreover, can make good sense if we understand them to have the distinctive capacity for initiating their own conduct rather than relying on mere stimulation and reaction. It also poses for them certain unique challenges, not the least of which is that they cannot reasonably expect any formula or system to predictably manage the future of human affairs, such as some of the social sciences seem to hope it will.

---

[10] John Rawls, *A Theory of Justice* (Cambridge: Harvard University Press, 1971), 104.

Social engineering is, thus, not a genuine prospect for solving human problems—only education and individual initiative can do that.

Yet, it should be noted that free will does not contradict social science if the latter is not conceived in strict deterministic terms and the former is understood to allow for long range commitments, chosen policies, strategies, institutional involvements, etc. Human beings make choices, some of which, however, commit them to a course of long range behavior which can be studied in terms of their impact on various features of the social world. People choose to enter schools, careers, relationships, to form institutions, to carry out plans, etc., and often their choices justify expecting them to stick with a reasonably predictable course of conduct.

In economics, for example, one may be studying the marketplace as an arena wherein human beings make various free choices concerning how they will be earning a living, what they will be producing and consuming, how they will be marketing their products, bargaining for prices, wages, and benefits, etc. The discipline examines the various permutations and consequences of these choices, as well as various regularities that are evident in the overall sphere of their activities.

Nonetheless, people are free to do what they do as commercial agents in various ways, embark upon their tasks more or less intensely at various periods of their lives, for various reasons of their own or because of circumstances they face. None of this needs to be determined by other than the individual agent and all these actions are open to moral evaluation.[11]

Yet this does not take away a good deal of orderliness, even predictability from people's economic activities, provided one does not expect that they behave like Haley's comet or a subatomic particle, according to impersonal laws or random forces. If social science appreciates that human beings have free will, they do not necessarily give up being scientific about human life, quite the contrary. And from human commitments, predictions about human behavior can become quite reliable though never along lines witnessed vis-à-vis mechanical processes.

1.21. Is the Free Will Idea "Spooky"?

In one of his famous books, Daniel Dennett asks, rhetorically of course:

> How does an *agent* cause an effect without there being an
> event (in the agent, presumably) that is the cause of that
> effect (and is itself the effect of an earlier cause, and so

---

[11] For more on this, see Tibor R. Machan, ed., *Commerce and Morality* (Lanham: Rowman and Littlefield, 1988), especially "Ethics and its Uses."

forth)? Agent causation is a frankly mysterious doctrine, positing something unparalleled by anything we discover in the causal processes of chemical reactions, nuclear fission and fusion, magnetic attraction, hurricanes, volcanoes, or such biological processes as metabolism, growth, immune reactions, and photosynthesis.[12]

First of all, the main argument for free will is no more mysterious than any arguments that rely on a dialectical move. If, as it turns out to be the case, free will is assumed even as one tries to deny it—in other words, the action of attempting to deny free will presupposes that the agent is capable of making original choices—that is sufficient to present a very strong case for free will. And the kind of independent thinking involved in argumentation does exactly that, namely, presuppose free will, the capacity to make choices, to take the initiative as a conceptually conscious agent. For what worth would any argument be if it merely amounted to a computational or genetic process? It would be no more compelling as argument as would be an "argument" advanced by a computer or parrot. The reason we can understand the reference to these as arguments is that we, human agents, can take them as such. But as products of computers or parrots they aren't arguments, only a bunch of sounds strung together.

Second, there is that aspect of the case for free will that relies on introspection. We often know about things this way, as when we answer our doctors very confidently about where we feel a pain in our bodies, or remember an event for which there is no evidence any longer apart from our memory. These are completely reliable kinds of knowledge and part of what gives us knowledge of our free will is that we are well aware of the fact that we often choose, initiate action, produce or create what we didn't have to produce or create. As I am writing the next few words in this discussion, I know at every moment I could stop, get up and get a soda from the fridge or continue with my project, as indeed I am choosing to do. Indeed, without this capacity the ideas of commitment to a project, tenacity, perseverance, ambition and such would be vacuous. And whatever one were to say on a subject, it would all be the result of various impersonal forces, never one's own initiative and self-determined close attention, good judgment or the like.

---

[12] Daniel Dennett, *Freedom Evolves* (New York: Viking, 2003), 100.

Finally, is Dennett's distinction between determinism and inevitability (or fatalism) sound? Let's look again at what he says:

> Inevitability means unavoidability, and if you think about what avoiding means, then you realize that in a deterministic world there's lots of avoidance. The capacity to avoid has been evolving for billions of years. There are very good avoiders now.[13]

Now suppose that I am typing along here and someone maintains that I am fully determined to do this.[14] I, however, in order to try to show that I am not, stop. Have I avoided some factors that were about to determine my continuing to type on? No, not according to determinism. Some other factors—such as, say, the presentation to me of the idea—well, the physical sounds that we take to indicate such an idea (although for materialist determinists the notion of an "idea" would be problematic without its being reducible to some matter or other) that I am determined, along with my psychological responsiveness to such a presentation—have come into play to redirect the anticipated flow of events, so that I am no longer typing along but stopping, reacting to these unanticipated but equally unavoidable factors or forces. Could I have done otherwise? Not according to the determinist view. Was it inevitable what happened? Surely, the presentation of the determinist's idea couldn't be avoided; my reaction couldn't either, and so on and so forth.

What Dennett takes to be a serious difference between determinism and fatalism is only a difference in how detailed a story one is going to tell. Sure, there is no fatalism of the sort where merely large movements proceed, unstoppably; but there is a fatalism of the sort where zillions of micro-movements interact in ways that even a humongous powerful computer might not predict exactly. Still, a sophisticated fatalist would rightly hold that whatever is going to happen, is fated to have happened, were all the details being fully, totally considered.

So, *pace* Dennett, if we know what avoidance means, we know that, paraphrasing him, "in a fatalistic world there's lots of avoidance." Why? Because what is called avoidance is a form of behavior that is determined

---

[13] Daniel Dennett, "Pulling Our Own Strings," Interview in *Reason Magazine* (May 2003).

[14] Perhaps the most detailed exploration of how determinism goes wrong here is offered in Ed Pols, *Acts of Our Being* (Amherst: University of Massachusetts Press, 1983).

to occur, just as any other form of behavior is determined to occur by way of the daisy chain of efficient causal links that connect the primordial past with the endless future (as per the picture determinists offer of reality).

What the agent causation position does not show, of course, is the *detailed correct or true full account of free will*, only that free will exists. Indeed, its existence is undeniable for us who are the acting agents. A detailed theory of agent causality would serve as an account of free will, not so much its proof.[15]

If such an account fails, however, perhaps the idea that we have free will has to be given a different account. But the issue we need briefly to consider is whether the agent causality account of free will *must* be unsound. That is the import of the claim, made by Dennett and others, that the very idea of agent causation is mysterious, spooky. When someone proposes that he has encountered a ghost, we tend to object not because of the belief that this particular ghost is unreal but because ghosts as such are impossible, their very idea is unfounded, baseless. And that is what the claim by Dennett & Co. concerning the mysteriousness of agent causality comes to. The idea is impossible.

But why is Dennett so confident that agent causation would have to be mysterious and thus impossible? Well, to answer we need to consider a famous argument about the nature of causality that occurred back in the eighteenth century.

It was David Hume who reasoned that if we depended for knowing the world entirely and solely on our sensory information, then causality itself must not be thought of as any kind of production or power. The billiard ball that strikes another and is taken, thus, to have made the other move has no (empirically) demonstrable productive powers at all. Instead, if we depend on our senses for knowledge, all we can justifiably claim is that the first billiard ball's motion was followed by that of the second, and *the oft-repeated instances of this result in our coming to gain the idea of causality*. (This is an odd move, by the way, since Hume is depending on a productive notion of causality to explain our belief in causality!) Regular or constant sequences like that are, for Hume, all that causes are, involving no evident causal *powers*.

Now the assumption that all of what we know comes from our senses is a pretty radical one and although Hume's idea of causality was very

---

[15] For a start on such an account, see Roger W. Sperry, "Changing Concepts of Consciousness and Free Will," *Perspectives in Biology and Medicine* 9 (August 1976): 9-19.

influential, most scientists and nearly all the rest of us did not fully accept his claim about causality because it rested on a radical empiricism that holds that all of what we know rests on nothing else but the contact our senses experience with input, input we cannot even be sure comes from anything outside our minds (brains). Yet many did accept a good deal of Hume's analysis of causation, so the idea that there can be something productive in a causal relationship has been dropped by most of those who think about causal connections in the world. It is this idea that is deemed to be spooky or mysterious by many because the productivity of a causal factor assumes something that is not directly evident—it isn't perceived by the senses. Instead it is inferred from the entire context of the causal situation.

So, for example, that the billiard ball has something about it—say, its solidity, its mass and density, that would produce an impact on another billiard ball so this other ball would be moved by it, is something that we do not see but infer. And although much of science welcomes direct evidence, first and foremost, as it considers convincing explanatory stories, science also makes room for inferred powers. For instance, black holes could not be detected by way of direct evidence for a long time, since by their very nature they didn't release any sensory information since their immense gravitational force did not allow such information, involving as it has to the emission of light, to escape for us to perceive it. So, the existence and nature of black holes were both discovered by inference, by noticing facts that could best be explained by the postulation of the black hole. (This is, of course, how the reality of many other beings are routinely established—for example, intentions, motives, wants, wishes, expectations, and so forth.)

In response to those like Dennett, then, who deny the possibility of agent causality—probably because they regard productive powers of causal factors as something mysterious or spooky—it needs to be stressed that such powers are not directly perceived but they can be inferred from other facts that can be perceived and our reflection on that fact. So, if the best explanation of what makes the second billiard ball move is that the first has certain properties—lacking in, say, a tennis ball—which can produce the typical movement in an entity such as the second ball, then that is a conclusion that is certain beyond a reasonable doubt (although not certain in the incorrigible, absolute sense Descartes' idea of knowledge, which Hume deployed for sensory impressions, would have required). Similarly, the power of human agents to be first causes can also be inferred along these lines. Given a certain composition of their brains, given the properties of them, and given the mental capacities—of, say, concept formation and self-reflection—they could well be the kind of beings capable of making original choices, of taking the initiative, just as we ordinarily believe they are.

II. MORAL SKEPTICISM

We now turn to the second assumption and briefly discuss the pros and cons.

Let's once again recall what's at stake: is there any basis for our ethical or moral judgments? When a politician is denounced, a newspaper criticized for its practices, or a teacher (or even a text book author) praised or blamed for his or her product, can any of this be made out? Is it possible to justify such judgments or claims? When one claims that one's parents have mistreated one or one's physician engaged in malpractice, is this just hot air or the expression of displeasure? Is it that we simply know this without any justification, without any basis for that knowledge? Is ethics, perhaps, some kind of realm where we can be right without any justification?[16] Or perhaps there are standards we can identify that can help us show that what we claim is true?

Our discussion, here, will again certainly not exhaust the topic. There is much more to be considered in a thorough study, but what we will do should help lay the foundation and give a clue as to what the debate involves.

2.1. Against Morality—Moral Diversity vs. Objectivity

There are too many moral opinions, so how can there be one, true moral standard for all? Clearly, across the globe and throughout human history great diversity exists and has existed concerning what is supposed to be right and wrong in human conduct. Indeed, apparently decent and intelligent people differ very seriously on the topic. Surely that suggests very strongly that no common, objective standard is available as to how we ought to act. It is mostly cultural anthropologists who advance this view—e.g., Ruth Benedict.[17]

---

[16] This view is advanced in the name of Ludwig Wittgenstein by Paul Johnston, *Wittgenstein and Moral Philosophy* (London: Routledge, 1989). But see, in contrast, Julius Kovesi, *Moral Notions* (London: Routledge & Kegan Paul, 1967), who also approaches ethics from a Wittgensteinian framework.

[17] Ruth Benedict, *Patterns of Culture* (Boston: Houghton Mifflin, 1934).

2.2. No Evidence of the Senses supports Moral Claims

Moral judgments are not verifiable by observation, as are many other judgments we make. We can pretty much decide what color hat one is wearing, how many people are sitting in a classroom, where China's borders are, how bright the sun is at noon, and other subjects we want to know about, by means of the diligent use of our sensory organs. Yet, no such use is going to enable us to decide whether we ought to tell the truth, write a letter to mother, help the poor, avoid pornography or ban abortions. Accordingly, moral disputes appear to be impossible to settle. This is an argument stressed by members of the philosophical school of logical positivism—e.g., A. J. Ayer.[18]

2.3. The Gap Between "Is" and "Ought"

No judgment of what is the case can support a conclusion of what one ought to do—the "is/ought" gap argument of the philosopher David Hume (1711–1776). The rules of sound reasoning, good judgment, require that when one draws a conclusion from premises, the terms that are present in this conclusion also appear in the premises. Yet if one begins an argument with claims about this or that being so and so, there is no "ought" or "should" present, whereas in a conclusion having moral import it is just those terms that would have to appear. Clearly, then, such moral conclusions cannot be derived from non-moral premises.

2.4. Morality is Against Nature

Nothing else in nature is subject to moral judgment or evaluation, so applying moral judgment or evaluation to human beings is odd, arbitrary, unjustified. Consider anything—rocks, trees, birds, fish or whatever, and there is no place for praising and blaming in our understanding of these things. So bringing morality into the picture when we consider human affairs is arbitrary, out of the blue, unjustified. John Mackie argues, for example, that moral values, if they existed, would be "entities or qualities or relations of a very strange sort, utterly different from anything else in the universe."[19]

2.5. For Morality—Diversity is More Apparent than Real

(A) Moral opinions tend to differ about details, not basics. (B) Some persons have a vested interest in obscuring moral standards lest they be found guilty of moral wrong doing or evil. (C) Some persons are professional

---

[18] A. J. Ayer, *Language, Truth and Logic* (New York: Dover, 1936).

[19] J. L. Mackie, *Ethics* (Baltimore: Penguin Books, 1977), 38.

"devil's advocates" and propagate skepticism because they are testing, questioning, making sure (even if they do not act as if they were skeptics, e.g., toward their children, friends, political reps).

2.6.Perceptual Knowledge is Not All

In complicated areas observations do not suffice to verify judgment—e.g., in astrophysics, particle physics, psychology, crime detection, etc. Moral judgments may require verification by way of a fairly complex theory or definition of, e.g., what "good" or "morally right" means. (Moral theories propose such theories and definitions.)

2.7. How not to Deduce but to Derive Ought from Is

(A) Hume was arguing against those who believed that moral conclusions can be deduced from premises stating various facts. But not all arguments consist of deductions, a formal statement linking premises to conclusions by nothing other than its logical structure and the essential meaning of the terms. Thus nothing strictly new is ever established by way of deduction, nothing that isn't true implicitly already. There is, however, reasoning that's not deductive but, roughly, inferential. Based on our observations, reflections, economical theorizing, and the like, we forge or develop an understanding of the world. When detectives explain a crime, they do not deduce—contrary to Sherlock Holmes—but infer who did it. Scientists work from evidence to conclusions in other than a strictly deductive fashion. They reach their understanding of what is what by developing valid, well founded concepts and theories that best explain what they see and have previously learned about. Indeed, most often we are concerned to establish definitions which are not the product of deduction but generalization, abstraction, the formation of ideas.

Accordingly, (B) the premises of moral arguments could include theories or definitions as to what "good" or "ought to" mean and thus give support to particular moral judgments. For example, "the will of God is Good," "Good is what everyone ought to do," thus, "the will of God is what everyone ought to obey." Or, "Goodness is Living (for human beings)," "Living (for human beings) is furthered by thinking," thus, "Goodness is furthered by thinking." These definitions or theories cannot be just dismissed. There is a possibility that one of them captures accurately what the relevant terms mean and from this we could infer moral conclusions.[20]

---

[20] For more along these lines, see W. D. Falk, *Ought, Reasons, and Morality* (Ithaca: Cornell University Press, 1986), especially "Goading and Guiding" and "Hume on Is and Ought."

2.8. Nature is Diverse Enough to allow for Major Differences

As in the case of the free will hypothesis, there is nothing odd about something new emerging in nature that does invite judgments. Mary Midgley puts forth a very interesting idea to the effect that human beings are precisely distinctive in the natural world by having a moral nature, a unique ethical dimension to their lives.[21]

Indeed, this view was advanced by Aristotle, as well.[22] It is evident enough, as well, as we consider how really extraordinary human life is—what other aspect of nature gives us board games, museums, symphony music, philosophy or the novel (as well as all the unsavory features. Such as murder, betrayal, ethnic cleansing, or embezzlement)?

THE BEST THEORY IS AS TRUE AS CAN BE

When we put all of this together what is at issue is whether we get a more sensible understanding of the complexities of human life than otherwise—do we get a better understanding, for example, of why social engineering and government regulation and regimentation do not work, why there are so many individual and cultural differences, why people can be wrong, why they can disagree with each other, etc. It may be because they are free to do so, because they are not set in some pattern the way cats and dogs and orangutans and birds tend to be. In principle, all of the behavior of these creatures around us can be predicted because they are not creative in a sense that they originate new ideas and behavior, although we do not always know enough about the constitution of these beings and how it would interact with their environment to actually predict what they will do. Human beings produce new ideas and these can introduce new kinds of behavior in familiar situations. This, in part, is what is meant by the fact that different people often interpret their experiences differently. Yet, we can make some predictions about what people will do because they often do make up their minds in a given fashion and stick to their decision over time. This is what we mean when we note that people make commitments, possess integrity, etc. So we can estimate

---

[21] Mary Midgley, *The Ethical Primate* (London: Routledge, 1994).

[22] Among others who advance a similar approach to ethics are Philippa Foot, Martha Nussbaum, and Ayn Rand (in *Natural Goodness* [New York: Oxford University Press, 2001], *The Therapy of Desire* [Princeton: Princeton University Press, 1996], and *The Virtue of Selfishness* [New York: New American Library, 1961], respectively).

what they are going to do. But even then we do not make certain predictions but only statistically significant ones. Clearly, very often people change their minds and surprise us. Furthermore, if we go to different cultures, they'll surprise us even more. This complexity, diversity, and individuation about human beings is best explained if human beings are free than if they are determined.

That is, at least, what is required for ethics to be a *bona fide*, genuine subject matter of concern.

HUMAN RIGHTS: A STEP BEYOND ENLIGHTENMENT
Francesco Viola

I wish to underline only one aspect of the different function of human rights today in connection with the Enlightenment yesterday. My point of view concerns the relationship between law, morals and politics. My opinion is that the development of the products of the Enlightenment has destroyed or at least denied the character of philosophy that was their source.

Usually one thinks that the Enlightenment does not know the historical dimension of human rights. In fact the Enlightenment's philosophy does not distinguish between natural and human rights and it has a rationalistic view of human nature. But the historical promulgation of natural rights introduces an element that little by little turns over the rationalistic conception. If human rights need promulgation, it means that this depends on human action. Natural rights become evident only owing to a revolutionary action, which destroys every obstacle of comprehension. This is not only a political and social action, but also an intellectual and cultural action. The promulgation belongs to the revolutionary activity. The misunderstanding by the Enlightenment was the identification between the principles of reason and their historical formulation. If this formulation is a revolutionary act, it is not a mere declaration of an eternal truth, but it implies an intervention of pragmatic character. From this point of view it is a cultural interpretation of human nature that is enforced by an act of will. The enlightened reason is in fact a practical reason, because it develops an interpretive activity and it commands. The Enlightenment's philosophy becomes praxis and it aims to transform a set of eternal truths into a social practice. But every social practice lives on the horizon of history. The enlightened reason claims also the role of an infallible legislator. But no one human legislator is infallible and neither is human reason. In the age of the French Revolution a statute of 1791 considered every trade-union and every strike as an attack against freedom and human rights. If human reason can be wrong, then the possibility of its correction must be opened. When the enlightened reason becomes a historical legislator, it must accept the contingency of its declarations and, therefore, the possibility of misunderstandings and errors; legislation is reformable. If human rights are objects of a legislative act, then they can change and develop too. Certainly the Enlightenment was not always conscious of this historical character of human rights, but surely it depends on the nature of the enlightened reason. The relevance of a declaration of human rights consists basically in this relationship between natural rights and history that the Enlightenment has introduced, but that its philosophy cannot suitably justify.

It might seem that the Enlightenment has neglected the historical dimension of human rights and it has considered them only from the point of view of their absoluteness. But it is not so. In effect the process of codification of human rights, that is a merit of the Enlightenment, constitutes their entry into history.

Therefore, as sons of the Enlightenment, human rights up to today have two faces, that produce their ambiguities. On one side, they are absolute and, on the other one, are historical. As principles they are of intrinsic worth, but they have also a history. Human rights change too; their list always grows greater, their content transforms itself profoundly.

Therefore we cannot think that the difference between our consideration of human rights and that of the age of Enlightenment is founded upon their rationalistic or historical dimension. We must look elsewhere. We must consider the relationship between the development of human rights and the philosophy of their justification. I wish to show that the increasing of the attention of positive law for human rights has contributed to the decline of legal theory as a theory of law's foundation.

The transformation of human rights into positive law has begun a development between law and morals that Bentham noted and vainly fought for. Morality has entered into law and tries to transform law in the moral sense; on the other side, law assumes a moral dignity, a moral force that is not external but internal. For some supporters legal positivism, that rejects every non-positive law, is interpreted also as an affirmation of legal self-sufficiency and, therefore, of moral autonomy.

In the aim of classic liberalism human rights were essentially a protection of the individual confronting of political power. For this reason they are properly natural rights, that is a "natural" obstacle to the arbitrary exercise of power. Their character was moral but not strictly juridical. The distinction between positive law and morals was saved. Natural law was not the place of foundation for positive law, but only an external limit of the content of positive law and of its exercise.

In the "Rechtsstaat" human rights have become the fundamental value of the state. They are fundamental rights and are included in the constitution. The legal positivity of human rights permits them to aim at the rôle of foundation for the whole legal system. Legal self-sufficiency asks that law is founded only by law. Now natural rights have become positive rights and therefore they can constitute an internal limit of government. Certainly the history of the "Rechtsstaat" is not so simple and it knows different interpretations that are bound to the formal or substantive character of human rights. But in every case the separation between law and morals is in jeopardy, if not cancelled.

In the "welfare state" human rights became goals of the state that is concerned with their substantive implementation. We can note that the development of historical determination of human rights has reached its extreme extension. A goal of a policy must be exactly determined from every point of view. This new formulation of human rights, that takes into account the particular situations of their respect, increases their contingency and their mutability. The variability of historical situations is transmitted to our way of thinking of human rights. Their list grows more and more as we can see in the recent declarations. But their universality and their immutability are more and more reduced. For every new policy of the state there is often a new interpretation concerning human rights. In this condition it is impossible to distinguish clearly between law, morals and politics. Consequently, the past function of foundation, that human rights had played, is practiced no more now.

Today the opposition between human rights and political power has failed. The state has completely digested these rights, at least in a theoretical sense. On the contrary the state tries to encroach on the sphere of personal liberties in a way that reminds one of political absolutism and paternalism. This development of human rights changes the relationship between law and morals in a relevant way.

When human rights were external limits of political power, their moral character was underlined, but not confused with the legal sphere. For the theoreticians of the French Revolution the cause of social evil was the ignorance of human rights. If they had been conveniently known, they would surely have been observed. For this reason it was necessary to have an official and public declaration. In this case the legal dimension of human rights is the smallest one. The accent is totally put on their proclamation, which enlightens minds and frees them of prejudices. The entry of human rights into the state produces a new situation in the relationship between morals, politics and law. On one side the morals must take into account political criteria; on the other one the law is confused with moral criteria.

An action is measured by a political criterion when it is considered a means to a goal. In this case the judgment does not concern the goodness of the goal, but the fitness of this action in attaining the proposed objective. An action is measured by a moral criterion, when it is considered as good or bad in itself. In this case the judgment concerns the intrinsic value of this action independently of its capacity to attain a goal.

When human rights become fundamental rights of the state, then they play the leading role of the policies' goals. But now these goals are internal to the state and are put on the same level as the fundamental political choices. Now human rights have the meaning of rules that measure the actions of the state as well as the general political principles—for example, the republican or monarchical form of government. But this choice is obviously reformable. If human rights are in force only when the state acknowledges them, then it also may not recognize them. The state may change its mind. If human rights take part in policies, then they are influenced by their changeability and inconstancy. This conclusion is necessarily derived from their entry into history, in particular when this history is that of the state.

On the other side, the total transformation of human rights into legal rights introduces a moral criterion in law. When the state submits itself to a criterion drawn from human rights, it accepts a moral guideline for action. If we abandoned the respect of human rights to the changeability of the policies, then no one universal declaration should have a meaning. A moral measure of an action must be delivered from every disposal of a will.

This confusion between morals, law and politics is not a prerogative of totalitarianism or of authoritarian government, but we also meet it in the "rule of law," albeit in a different way. The present situation is very far from the intentions of the enlightened man, who tries to maintain distinct fields of practical experience. But one can note that this development was implicit in the act of promulgation of human rights. These wear the clothes of history, they become legal rights, and they acquire a specific articulation. Nevertheless they try to maintain their rôle of criterion of evaluation that requests a detachment from the other legal rights not only by way of the position, but also by way of the existence.

In conclusion, the two horns of the dilemma are as follows: if human rights have the function of criteria of evaluation or of legitimacy of the state, they must be different from what is valued as the ancient natural law was different. If human rights are intended as internal criteria of the legislative action, they must become totally positive or at least must have a high degree of articulation in a determinate formulation. Thus every theory of legal (or moral) foundation is subject to two contradictory exigencies: the criteria of foundation must be internal to what is founded, otherwise the specificity of law will not be preserved; on the other hand, these criteria must be different from the system they support, otherwise the question is not solved.

We have seen that human rights are internal to law now, but we have also noted that their formulation always looks more like the other norms of legal system and the more changeable pieces of it as, for example, the policies. Meanwhile the modern natural law did not permit a self-sufficient foundation of positive law; the contemporary human rights do not permit a foundation at all, because they are too much confused with the other elements of a juridical system. But nobody can deny that today human rights constitute the indisputable basis of the political legitimacy and of international relationships.

My opinion is that there is only one way to save the foundational function of human rights in the contemporary situation. One must accept that inside a legal system not every normative formulation has the same value and neither must every norm be considered in the same way. The formulation of a legal (or moral) principle is only a contingent expression that does not grasp totally the potentiality of a value. A legal system is not only composed of the actual formulations of principles but also of all the possible formulations as a symphony contains all its performances beside the actual execution.

We do not know totally the juridical system, but always its determinate configuration in a determinate historical position. We can know only a performance of positive law and we discuss whether this is more or less correct, more or less 'right', as well as we ask whether a performance of a symphony is more or less accurate. Accurate as to what? Right as to what? Certainly, not as an eternal model of natural law and neither as a contingent codex of positive rules. For asking these questions the model of the Enlightenment must be abandoned.

Law must not be prefigured under the appearance of a text or of a set of norms or decisions now, but basically as a social practice. To know the

law of a determinate human community shall mean to describe a complicated social practice that has its identity but is continuously changeable.
The specificity of a social practice is its *potential dimension* that is its
inexhaustibility in front of the concrete applications, its capacity of fitness
and for transformation. In a word not all is given in a practice, but it is
necessary to exercise a "creative" interpretation, that is such in front of the
data but not of the profound soul and identity of practice itself.
Therefore the interpretive attitude belongs to the process of knowledge of
a social practice.

I may not dwell on the conception of law as social practice that today
however spreads always more. Here I wish to note only that its possibility
depends on the presence in a legal system of something that is not
exhausted by the contingent formulations, on the presence of fundamental
values as human rights. If a legal system has not a hidden part as an
iceberg, it has not its identity and therefore cannot face the transformation.
It has no roots. This means also that the criterion of evaluation is internal
to the system itself, but at the same time it goes beyond its different
expressions. Alike we value correctly a masterpiece through aesthetic
criteria drawn from its inside and not through external canons that seldom
permit the appreciation of the new forms of beauty.

If it is so, then a declaration of man's and citizen's rights is not their
definition. It is nothing but their authoritative interpretation, to which one
can assign a historical relevance but non-conclusive. This is not the
attitude of the Enlightenment, but the totally opposite point of view; the
hermeneutic point of view. This question cannot be solved on the basis of
the Enlightenment's philosophy, but requires a hermeneutic approach.

For a social practice does not really exist without the concrete acts of
application, the problem of its foundation puts itself in a totally different
way. It is not the question to prove the existence of something called 'law'
as separated or distinguished by other similar things as morals or politics.
It is the question of justifying actions and interpretive acts now. The juridical
foundation wears the clothes of the legal justification now. The distinction
between law, morals and politics does not concern a distinction of objects
but of interpretive processes and of reasons in balance. The equivocal
character of human rights, that are *moral rights* as goals of policies, can
avoid the confusion in practical criteria only on the level of justification,
which must belong to legal theory in every respect, contrary to Kelsen's
opinion. Also, from this aspect legal theory must abandon the proper

attitude of the Enlightenment that has found its way into the culture of codification and into the separation thesis between law and morals.

In conclusion, one can affirm that the Enlightenment, which has produced human rights in the modern sense, has led the way to a process that brings legal theory far from the enlightened conception of law. When Bentham fought against the concept of human rights ("nonsense upon stilts"), he perspicaciously located one of the enemies of the Enlightenment's legal culture. He does not refute their content, but rather their formulation itself.

MONEY, DEMOCRACY, AND THE GOOD LIFE
Timothy D. Sullivan

In ancient cultures, economy originates with the family and under a religious aegis. In the polis a coin bore the stamp of a common god. Money, like all equally valid concepts of measure—for example, weight, size, and time—in ancient societies emanated from priesthood. Even the value relations between precious metals could be based upon relations between the planets, for they were divinities. There were periods when the commercial ratio of gold to silver (1: 13 ½) was based upon the relation between the lengths of the lunar and solar courses (27: 360).[1] No such connection could be assigned now between money, precious metals, planets, or divinities. It was possible in the past because the *theion* was present in the cosmos, and the presence of the divine in the cosmic order was reflected in the order of the polis and in the order of the household. But we live in space amidst matter without the directionality of an ordered cosmos.

In the ancient economy, the household is a community of persons. Like the wider community it is not a collection of individuals, but an ordered whole. These ordered wholes are bound together by mutuality.[2] They perceive their associations along the lines of kinship and the sacred. In that view, the world of the market and money making can be anarchical.[3] This is the case since money and exchange absorb goods into the economy where the goods are then valued for the money they can bring through exchange—that process is said to denature goods, for they are valued not as goods, but in terms of money.[4] When the dynamism of the economic element enters into communal life, then mutuality may become problematic. We have a tension between a community without commerce which can incur poverty, and the interdependencies to which

---

[1] Eric Voegelin, *Order and History,* Vol. 2, *The World of the Polis* (Baton Rouge: Louisiana State University Press, 1957), 151.

[2] William James Booth, "Household and Market: On the Origins of Moral Economic Philosophy." *The Review of Politics,* Vol. 56, no.2 (Spring 1994), 211.

[3] Ibid., 213.

[4] Ibid., 214.

trade and commerce can lead, until finally the polis is not its own master. From the point of view of the well ordered community this is inimical to its own good.

In particular, at the end of the sixth century, Athens was entering such a period. What would have been unthinkable, not only unspeakable, became theater. Colonies were established, international trade flourished, and wealth increased. Socially and culturally Athens was being transformed into a commercial and military power whose fortunes no longer were based only on land, herds, booty or slaves. Trade, colonies, shipping and exchange offered new avenues of accumulation and profit. Athens had money, and like our money it was a cultural artifact; but it was not abstract. Our money is abstract; it has become more than an instrument of commerce, and more than a "game of its own," as it presently is in the speculative tier of the economy.

A contemporary economy need not see its money as bearing the symbol of the common good. It is a money sufficiently abstract to seem unaffected by time and place. While it exists in the form of numbers, and moves without heed of distance, it simultaneously can be a determining standard of both the political and economic spheres. It exists not only in currency and coin, but in the form of mediating exchanges and measuring value. Indeed, money exists properly in these ways and almost accidentally as currency and coin. Like language, this does not exist in the alphabet or the lexicon, but in expression and in exchanges. In the interior dialogue, money like language is an instrument of thought. Just as one's thoughts must take the form of a "universally" understood language, so must one's activities and possessions take the form of money value in order to serve one's remote purposes.[5] Money validates one's possessions and expresses one's wealth. To think about them apart from money is possible, but it is thought that does not contemplate action.

At present money masks a subjective process. Economic objects are handed over to a process of exchange in which labor, costs of the factors involved, and preferences do not circumscribe the objects of value. They confront the individual as a given operative realm, but this realm is not reducible to the useful or the pleasurable. Objects and services may be said to circulate according to norms and measures that are fixed at any moment in what Simmel calls an objective supra-personal

---

[5] Georg Simmel, *The Philosophy of Money*, trans. T. Bottomore and D. Frisby (London: Routledge and Kegan Paul, 1978), 210.

relationship between objects.[6] These objects are encapsulated in a mechanism of exchange that derives values from the relation between objects.[7] An economy founded on the relationships implicit here is always tending toward a stage of development which is neither completely achieved nor unrealized. In this system of exchange there is no objective good or value.[8] Their presence would mean the interference of the individual object as content based value in a system that derives value from the relation between objects. In this objective, supra-personal relationship between objects a person can only participate as a representative or executor of determinants which lie outside him. With that tension, and in that sense, exchange is a form of life; and money becomes a passage to the interpretation of existence. Money is able to become more and more a symbol of economic value because economic value is nothing but the relativity of exchange objects. This relativity, in its turn, increasingly dominates the other qualities of the objects that serve as money. The concept of money is all but cut loose from objects while at the same time it becomes a concise expression of the economic value of things. It is the growing spiritualization of money.[9] Its concept becomes ever more abstract.

Such money, in its psychological form, possesses a significant relationship to the notion of God.[10] Simmel cites Hans Sachs to the effect that money is the secular God of the world.[11] The essence of this money lies in its being the absolute means, and thereby becoming psychologically the absolute purpose for most people. This makes it a symbol in which the main regulators of practical life are frozen; while being abstract it becomes a presence in the lives and decisions of all society's classes. In this psychological and metaphysical form money has or represents omnipotence.[12] When the religious absolute, as the ultimate purpose of

[6] Ibid., 79.

[7] Ibid., 127.

[8] The medieval tradition of substantive justice, intrinsic value, and just price changed. Between 1790 and 1850 the emphasis in legal and economic thought was on the random and fluctuating nature of value that had been introduced by a market economy. Morton J. Horwitz, *The Transformation of American Law, 1780–1860* (Cambridge: Harvard University Press, 1977), 160-161, 196-200.

[9] Simmel, op. cit., 198.

[10] Ibid., 236.

[11] Ibid., 237-238.

[12] Ibid., 237.

existence, has lost its power, acquisitiveness is at its height. While it is always present, it is only then that money has or represents omnipotence. Money becomes a concrete means which is identical with its abstract concept. Such a measure and expression is not possible until the society has achieved a level of life-interpretation which allows its experiences to be organized in harmony with the interests of commercial life. In a society based on the ethos of money, human actions are performed, as human affairs are conducted, under the aegis of money. It will receive different names depending upon circumstances. At one time it would be cost, at another the budget, or savings, or consumption, or debt, income, expense, so many abstractions. Free formed by thought they constitute the categories of thought. According to the weightiness of these categories money is not content with being just another final purpose of life alongside wisdom, art, personal significance, strength, beauty and love. In so far as it is the standard for everything else it gains the power to reduce the other purposes to the level of means.[13] Wisdom is a way to obtain money; art is a means to obtain money; and love is a way to money.

The market economy may make this order of things difficult to avoid. In addition, while money and markets are accomplishing these changes to the characters of men in the economic sphere, democracy can conflate with them in the political sphere.[14] At present they have become complementary paradigms. Indeed, if the global economy is to be an actuality overall, there is a need for parliamentary democracies, published budgets, and a legal code covering contracts and property rights. The two developments have been part of the growth of societies that are predominantly market societies. Democracy is a means since it allows for parliamentary institutions which in turn marshal budgets and revenues. These are necessary in a society where the economic actors are unknown to one another, and their relationship cannot be based on trust or confidence in the moral probity of others in the marketplace; at least not beyond a limited circle. Trust, therefore, has to be based upon procedures which are protected by political and juridical means. The emphasis on democracy and parliamentary institutions allows for public knowledge of procedures, and so allows markets to be based on the actions of free individuals engaging in exchange. The promotion and extension of democracy, therefore, is synonymous with constitutional, legal and

[13] Ibid., 241.

[14] Booth, op. cit., 228.

financial guarantees for citizens, and guarantees also for commerce, finance and trade. The resultant economic order is an appendage, or booster, for *homo economicus* and forms of economic *ratio*, namely creeds which welcome self-interest, utility, and the pursuit of wealth. Such moral orders are complementary to their economies, but alone they cannot justify the "way of life" which we have described earlier.

There is no philosophical—as opposed to ideological or economic—reason for supposing that such an order is not marked by disorder. Consisting as it does of money and markets of supra-personal objects, it sucks in persons and populations under the shell of the money *imperium*; with it come the depersonalization of society and the commodification of persons, and there is no way to avoid this.[15] The reduction of the concrete values of life to a means, and their subordination to the mediating value of money sees its results in cynicism and a blasé attitude. Disparaging all old values, a money economy's ethos is determinative of human character. Neither the concrete values of life nor valuations rooted in tradition are sufficiently established to displace the influence on conduct of the money economy. Side by side, conscience by conscience, often within the same individual, two modes of conduct are in tension. One attempts to order itself within an order of objective good; for it an absolute good exists, and other goods reflect it, or are a means to it, or both. The second mode of conduct is not governed by an objective good, nor is it directed by the inner worth of persons, things, or thoughts. Such people, if only interested in money, achieve the quality of characterlessness.[16] Whenever genuine personal values have to be offered for money without any further non-material compensation, one finds that a loosening, almost a loss, of substance in the individual takes place.[17] It is the loss of character. The fact that life is no longer determined by the distinctiveness of character is the life-style. It is apparent in the peculiar level of emotional life ascribed to contemporary times; it contrasts with the forthrightness and ruggedness of earlier epochs.[18]

This general economic culture is what will accompany the growth of a global economy. In the circumstances we have described, it will be

---

[15] Robert Heilbroner, *Visions of the Future: The Distant Past, Yesterday, Today, Tomorrow* (New York: Oxford University Press, 1995), 99.

[16] Simmel, op. cit., 216.

[17] Ibid., 407.

[18] Ibid., 432-433.

leavened by the omnipotence of money. As a consequence, individually and collectively, the members of a society understand that their specific money interests are a determining influence in their decisions. Reason, therefore, can become an instrument, often a weapon, to be employed in attaining goals in their mutual dealings. Such a society is what is left after community has been ravished by the power drive which exploits both for the sake of real wealth and also financial wealth. A market economy becomes in large part a money society.

To reduce human affairs to questions of money, namely, cost, expense, debt, profit, loss is in practice a denial of any other order than wealth itself. When it is combined with the knowledge of the social sciences and statistics, it becomes an ideology. If it is extended still further to become an explanation of history as moving along a line of material progress, it has become a dream. In so far as its focus is towards the further, that is, tomorrow, it proffers an object of belief, but the mélange of money, facts, statistics, ideology and belief, are not a scientific knowledge, nor are they susceptible to testing other than by the rhetor's points in debate. We have pseudo-knowledge in the service of money. To the idolatry of times when men stood, knelt, or prostrated themselves before objects of stone, clay, or wood is added the idolatry extended towards money.

In the name of rationality such a societal order exercises a formative influence on the conditions of life, reproduction, and death: science and technology intrude into personal and daily life.[19] This is evident in occupational structures and birth rates. The coercive power of money, however, is often felt in the harshest terms by the peoples of those nations subject to international banking and credit practices. Programs and policies applied in such circumstances appear as rational choices, but to those who are thus organized they can appear as oppression. The problem for an order of global capital and global exchange is that the reasons for a life lived in common can be reduced to those of an organization of people to promote trade and commerce on the one hand, and to prevent crime on the other. Perhaps as a paradigm for piranha that would suffice; but persons pursuing self interest without a moral paradigm are in the odd situation of being anti-social. Any social order, including a global economic order, has to have a paradigm within which it can balance the insolence and criminality which accompany excessive wealth, and the malice and roguery bred by poverty.

---

[19] Heilbroner, op. cit., 99.

But according to the intellectual premises of such a society the exploitation and transformation of the material world, and the accumulation of capital, are the sole purposes of money and markets; and this in a world devoid of a religious absolute as the ultimate ordering purpose of individual and social life. It marshals and expends its energies in pursuit of capital. This expansion is the life process of the system. Otherwise competition would erode profits and capitalists would have no incentive for investment.[20] In such a system people can find their norms, purposes, and valuations in terms of money. The good is to be found in money, and money becomes the empirical symbol in this objective life-style of the conceivable unity of being out of which the world and reality flow.[21] Such a societal order can appear irreversible.

Analytically, the concepts, or the propaganda, which represent portions of the shared knowledge individuals have of one another in such a society are not immediately intelligible. As when we have a drop in the rate of unemployment, then there is danger of inflation; when unemployment rises consumer confidence may wane, or consumer spending drop, or both. All news is bad news. If corporations reveal plans to lay off workers in order to reduce costs, the value of their shares may increase. When corporations start to hire, there may be a shortage of skilled workers, and therefore full efficiency cannot be realized. If food prices rise consistently, it is inflation. If the prices of publicly traded shares rise in a similar way, it is an increase in value; these "truths" risk being ideological slogans. Through it all there is an exclusion of the lives of persons; their three-score ten of growth, family, children, their personal destinies, are not a question. By excluding all that is personal, all that pertains to the drama and to the tragic in the lives of those affected by such trends, the markets are able to focus solely on money. It is a methodology which leaves us with a picture of people unable to think in other terms than economic ones.

This is done under the leadership of a new social type.[22] They have their own form of thinking which is nominalist, and the method is critical not intuitive. It is the transformation of intuitive intellect into the technically relevant "understanding" of a newer experimental and mathematical

[20] Ibid.

[21] Simmel, op. cit., 497.

[22] Max Scheler, *Problems of a Sociology of Knowledge*, trans. Manfred S. Frings (Boston: Routledge and Kegan Paul, 1980), 124-125.

naturalism. These are not just forms of thought. More importantly, they are forms of experience. As they are newer forms of experience older forms will break up, with the result that the prior organization of natural objects and values, of causes and purposes, begins to fall apart; and a theory of objective values is replaced by subjective needs. One witnesses politically and economically active individuals seeking to rectify the social and moral lexicon within a framework de-cultivated of religion and the spirit. It is this new universe of discourse which evaluates life and reproduction while recasting debate in terms of sustainable populations and individual choice. The state authority in particular is required to be democratic and egalitarian rather than hierarchical and representative of an establishment, but the money *imperium* and the aggregates of capital are class-leavened and pyramid-like.

With this as a point of departure one reflects upon the problems of production-consumption, investment-return, and constitution-legislation; but that does not speak to the issues that have brought down empires: the clash between the haves and the have-nots, the rulers and the ruled, the urban and the rural populations. No one says they have a solution for these conflicts, but economically and politically active individuals will seek to control populations, to manage their size, and willy-nilly draw to urban areas the rural populations, often under the rubric of free enterprise. The formative influence of this "way of life" is incorporated in the social and economic ordering of lives of work, consumption, entertainment, and distraction; and these in turn are coupled with the need for money, for wealth, if one is to partake of the dream. The resultant respect for money is such that this "way of life" can hardly avoid being corrosive of any norms not harmonizable with accounting principles. Indeed, it exercises its own totalitarian influence over noetic life to the point where it is difficult for many people to think in other categories.

If the aspirations of the global economy are not untracked by future events, and even if they are, it is a question as to why such a global economy should be a goal. In addition to its exclusion of objective norms, the potential material gains will all bring dilemmas with them: a longer life for many brings an aging population; globally increasing production and consumption bring problems of depletion and destruction of the earth; there is the precise problem of capitalism's dynamic growth which is achieved by the destruction of industries as well as of resources; and then there is the problem of kinship ties in money societies, which ties have been altered or made obsolete to an extent that we who live in such societies can hardly appreciate. In other words, if a global economy were to avoid problems of the distribution of wealth, problems of haves versus have-nots, of rulers versus the ruled, of the concentration of the earth's population in cities, if it were in some extraordinary way to incorporate the peoples of the earth under a global economic *imperium*, it would thereby create the conditions of its own deterioration. If one could predict that this disorder passing for order would collapse, perhaps one could ignore the problem. But aside from the principle that things have a beginning and an end, it is not necessary that its deterioration be identical with its collapse or disappearance. Something, in a sense, worse might befall those under its *imperium*. If structures of control and organization grow while the coarsening of moral sensibilities continues, what that can mean is the continuation of the present threat. Namely, that men and women will lose any conception of the excellence of character which results from human growth noetically and morally.

This is the culture of consumer capitalism and it is non-consensual in origin and in its exclusion of other views of the good life.[23] It becomes more and more ubiquitous, for money and markets are universal. They homogenize things and persons rendering them the same, and removing them from any natural place in family, kinship, and tradition; for in a real sense money and markets are homeless; and therefore they are antithetical to the mutuality proper to social life. The membership of human beings in an ordered community is made mute.[24] Of this state of things the view has been expressed that it is the oppressive market which rules us, not an oppressive state.[25] Its culture requires all, to different degrees, to participate in an acquisitive life.[26] They are serious about life and its pleasures, but not about the good life. But societies based predominantly upon economic development criteria risk having no *raison d'être* beyond their investment and production schedules. For this culture, the market economy is at one and the same time a series of exchanges between free individuals, and an organization of the *nomoi* according to which free individuals choose. The market economy, therefore, forms a social order whose moral consciousness arises not out of custom, or myth, or revelation, but finally

---

[23] David C. Korten, *When Corporations Rule the World* (West Hartford: Kumarian Press, 1995), 150-151.

[24] Booth, op. cit., 213.

[25] Korten, op. cit., 157.

[26] Booth, op. cit., 214.

out of the money *imperium*. It is by the instrumentality of the judiciary, as well as legislation, that this change has proceeded.

Legal relations that were once conceived of as deriving from natural law or custom were increasingly subordinated to economic development. Law once thought of as the expression of the moral sense of the community, came to be regarded as a reflection of the existing organization of economic and political power.[27] Money is in the foreground, other valuations are in the background. Therefore, the market economy in serving needs and providing for the availability of goods and services not only establishes a remarkable organization of investment, production, communication and exchange. At the same time, it organizes the relations of productive property to society. In doing so, market economies have transformed the nature and the meaning of property, and therefore of wealth. Property has become a bundle of legal relations not necessarily describing any res at all: property has become a bundle of rights, of immunities, of powers, of privileges.[28] Property has become abstract. Today's financial instruments exemplify this while testifying to the role of intellect in the production and creation of wealth. Therefore what the money *imperium* is actually doing, as distinct from what it says it is doing, is seen in the difference between establishing liberty under law, and arriving at laws establishing economic imperatives. In legal history, commercial law, and jurisprudence, there have been adjustments whose intent was to further the social conditions which are indispensable for economic development to occur. The evolution of law has been, for the most part, proceeding according to a functional rationality.[29] Legal theory and philosophy, for example, in the late nineteenth and early twentieth century were breaking with theological and doctrinal modes of thought.[30] By the 1960s, there was one trend in legal thought, at the University of Chicago, which held that law should be based on the efficient operation of the marketplace. Behind this lay classical economic theory.[31] Free choice, therefore, is qualified by the *imperium* of money.

---

[27] Horwitz, op. cit., 253. Kermit L. Hall, *The Magic Mirror* (New York: Oxford University Press, 1989), p. 79.

[28] Morton J. Horwitz, *The Transformation of American Law, 1870–1960* (New York: Oxford University Press, 1992), 156.

[29] Ibid., 130.

[30] Ibid., 142, and Max Scheler, *Le Formalisme en Éthique* (Der Formalismus in der Ethik), trans. Maurice de Gaudillac (Paris: Gallimard, 1955), 305-318 (306-320).

[31] Horowitz, op. cit., 212-227.

It is not possible, however, to justify a market society or a global economy on the basis that commerce and industry are the terminal purposes of human life. Human nature does not change. Something else is required, and that something else will be superior to money. Is democracy that which is superior? Freedom, of course, is what democracies originally intend; but the freedom of the market society has the conditions and limitations indicated above. Alternatively, if democracies overtly and authoritatively set a moral goal, the secular state would have reversed its own role in a market economy. Something that is superior to democracy and to money is still required; but to admit it and not merely nod at it would require a reordering of ends and means in the social economy, and this to the point where the personal, the familial, and the sacred would not simply keep out of the way of material progress. The questioning of material progress, however, is not a lesson easily assimilable along the highway of super-greed. The combination of respect for the rule of money, and the subordination of higher ends and purposes to its rule is a rejection of a greater for a lesser good.

In practice, the global hegemony of capital and commerce form a shell over peoples of diverse cultures and also over different civilizations. Its dynamism can disrupt or destroy "ways of life," customs, and conventions. Inevitably it can displace what William James called the furniture of the mind in which each of us is a conservative. Intrastate conflicts, international conflicts, and those between civilizations, therefore, do not exhaust the fields of power relations; and while they can disrupt and destroy they have so far presumed a victor as well as a vanquished. However, global domination by money and markets, inadequately tempered by justice, within a universe of matter indifferent to human ends, leave us an anthill. Democracy and freedom are the symbols justifying this as the good life. Spengler had a point in maintaining that democracy is the wish but plutocracy is the fact. Plato experienced it as the feverish polis, and Socrates railed against those who gave Athens its docks but had forgotten what was greater; for in Athens the gods had died, and without a dialogue with the gods Athens had no reason to exist. We have on the one hand the "busy life," and on the other the human purposes of life organized around ultimate goals. These are the centrifugal and centripetal movements of human affairs.

Of course, much of the world reaps little or no advantage from money, markets or democracy. The potential extension of their advantages to those billions of people would be a benefit in terms of health and the "standard of living," but it would mean that the legal order governing social relations will change; and with that change will come either a new occupational structure or one transformed. The result is a new social order which on its reverse side is a new moral order, for money and markets bring their own formative lessons. Not a little of what was formerly part of many lives will be gone, some of it happily, some of it to their loss. Mass societies, by definition, level structures which formerly sustained communal life. Minus that support alienation can be endemic. No small part of it is caused by conflicts arising out of the self-interest which results from the newer forms of social and economic organization. In addition, the calculative reason of the bureaucracies of business, education, and government is predisposed to evaluate social, political, and economic questions within the framework of the secular state. Given the sensate culture of the latter, the reduction of spiritual or moral questions to ones of individual utility or pleasure is a strong tendency.

Such a tendency originates in the change of value-ception which accompanies the presence of a new social type. The term value-ception is that of Scheler. It refers to the experience of values in a natural and social world. The values are a given; the feasibility of the values and their symbols vary.[32] Value-ception, therefore, has an objective content. This is something that positivism, the theory of science, and behaviorist ideology has rejected: the evidence of experience and the given-ness of its value are subjectivized. Against this background the calculative reason of market societies either discounts value-ception or, where it recognizes values, makes all values equal. In this way, the values of utility, well being, and comfort are on a par with the experience of the sacred, the appreciation of beauty, and a sense of what is honorable. The former values are those in which we are most alike; the latter are those which, even in being shared, are marked by our individual differences. The result is an indifference regarding some of the consequences of an expanding money *imperium*, particularly, a conscious exclusion of those experiences which challenge the leveling of moral conduct. The good life seems left to be defined by the age, and those whose formation is in keeping with its social and cultural dynamics. The century's long development of market economies has bred its leadership and readied its guidelines. In communications, education, law, politics, as well as commerce, these are the dominant *nomoi*. The link between economic development and a new social type

---

[32] Scheler, op. cit., 127.

with its value-ception results in the good life understood as excellence of character, the inculcation of virtue, and an acknowledgment of order and subordination among values becoming unintelligible, even indefensible. Standards can become illusory. It is this latter condition which could contribute to the diverse cultures and the social and moral orders, in which markets must at present operate, becoming tractable for the money *imperium*.

Money has been transformed, as have constitutional democracy, jurisprudence, and the good life. The latter has been reduced to a consumer paradise. Democracy, as freedom under the rule of law, has been reduced to a state in which money often rules politics, which is a case of the "tail wagging the dog." There is a literature that deals with the measures governments can take in coping with a global economy. They have the power to make laws and to enforce them, if they choose to do so; the tax system can assuage the disruptive effects of capital movement. There is a need, therefore, for political sovereignty to assert itself, if money power is not to become a new form of despotism. A balance between the dynamism of economic development and the good of the social order is required in order that an alternative justification for a life lived in common is not lost in oblivion, a justification other than that of expanding markets and accumulating capital. Of course there are financial disasters which can overtake market economies and provide "incentives" for corrections. Even with that the question remains, is the contemporary identification of the good life with enjoyment and possessions sufficiently desiccative of conscience and one's sensibilities that servitude could be the result?

BOOK REVIEW

JOHN LOCKE'S MORAL REVOLUTION: FROM NATURAL LAW TO MORAL RELATIVISM

By Samuel Zinaich, Jr.
University Press of America, 2006

Reviewed by Peter P. Cvek
Department of Philosophy, Saint Peter's College

The status of John Locke as a natural law theorist has been especially problematic for contemporary scholars. On the one hand, in the *Two Treatises of Government* (1690), Locke appears to expound a political philosophy rooted in the traditional theory of natural law. Locke employed the normative language of natural law discourse and expressed his debt to Richard Hooker, the Anglican proponent of a Thomistic conception of natural law. On the other hand, many readers of the *Essay Concerning Human Understanding* (1690) have suggested that Locke's epistemology, despite his protestations to the contrary, was more compatible with some version of moral relativism than with any theory of natural law. Leo Strauss took this controversy to another level, arguing that Locke's use of traditional language and sources in the *Two Treatises* was intended to conceal his real sympathies with the philosophy of Hobbes.[1] The debate took yet another twist when W. von Leyden published *Essays on the Law of Nature*, a series of essays on natural law written by Locke between 1660 and 1664.[2] For many scholars, the existence of these *Essays* strengthened the image of Locke as a lifelong proponent of natural law. For others, including Strauss, the alleged inconsistencies in the text supported their "Hobbes in disguise" reading of Locke.[3] In his *John Locke's Moral Revolution: From Natural Law to Moral Relativism*, Samuel Zinaich has decided to split the difference.

---

[1] Leo Strauss, *Natural Right and History* (Chicago: University of Chicago Press, 1953), 202-251.

[2] Locke's early writings on the natural law are in ten essays, which were edited and translated by W. von Leyden, under the title *Essays on the Law of Nature*, (Oxford: Clarendon Press, 1954). All references to this work will be provided within parentheses in the body of the text and listed by page and folio number.

[3] Leo Strauss, "Locke's Doctrine of Natural Law," in *What is Political Philosophy? And other studies* (Chicago: University of Chicago Press, 1959), 197-220.

According to Professor Zinaich, John Locke, as exemplified in his *Essays on the Law of Nature*, was initially committed to the Christian natural law tradition. More specifically, Zinaich argues that in the *Essays* Locke embraced an Aristotelian-Thomistic world-view, which includes three major elements: a reliance on Aristotelian essentialism, a classical view of virtue and vice, and a firm belief in moral absolutism. But by the time he published *An Essay Concerning Human Understanding*, Locke had abandoned essentialism in favor of the corpuscular philosophy and, as a consequence, he rejected the classical conception of virtue and vice in favor of a hedonistic theory of good and evil, and replaced moral absolutism with moral relativism. While this reading of the *Essay* is not unprecedented, it is Zinaich's interpretation of the *Essays* that is the more novel aspect of his study and it certainly enhances the dramatic character of Locke's moral revolution. Since the major theme of Zinaich's work is the radical contrast between the moral philosophies advanced in these two texts, I will examine each of his arguments in turn.

Zinaich's defense of his traditionalist reading of the *Essays* is based primarily on the first of Locke's essays entitled "Is There a Rule of Morals, or Law of Nature Given to us? Yes." In this essay, Locke expounds five arguments aimed at demonstrating the existence of the law of nature. Although Zinaich critically discusses each of these arguments, the first and the third arguments are crucial to his interpretation. To begin with the third, Locke states:

> [T]he third argument is derived from the very constitution of the world, wherein all things observe a fixed law of their operations and a manner of existence appropriate to their nature. For that which prescribes to every thing the form and manner and measure of working is just what law is. Aquinas says that all that happens in things created is the subject mater of the eternal law, and, following Hippocrates, 'each thing both in small and in great fulfilleth the task which destiny hath set down,' that is to say nothing deviates even by an inch from the law prescribed to it (117, f. 18).

According to Zinaich, the third argument illustrates Locke's acceptance of the Aristotelian world-view, including the belief in substantial forms and final causality, while the reference to Aquinas and eternal law reflects his commitment to the Christian natural law tradition. This intellectual framework assumes that man has a prescribed mode of action that is suited to his nature, since it would be incompatible with God's wisdom to have created humanity without assigning to human beings a proper function or purpose (37). The first argument simply looks to Aristotle for the identity of that proper function:

> [T]he first argument can be derived from a passage in Aristotle's *Nicomachean Ethics*, Book I, chapter 7, where he says that 'the special function of man is the active exercise of the mind's faculties in accordance with rational principle.' For since in the preceding passages he had shown by various examples that there is a special sort of work each thing is designed to perform, he tried to find out what this may be in the case of a human being also. Thus, having taken account of all the operations of the vegetal and sentient faculties which men have in common with animals and plants, in the end he rightly concludes that the proper function of man is acting in conformity with reason, so much so that man must of necessity perform what reason prescribes (113, f. 13).

Professor Zinaich correctly notes that "the reader must not assume that just because Locke has two Aristotelian arguments at the beginning of his discussion that this automatically put the *Essays* within this tradition."[4] Zinaich adds that there is much evidence within the text itself to demonstrate Locke's reliance on Aristotelian essentialism and his acceptance of the Christian tradition of natural law. Unfortunately, what appears to be this additional evidence either begs the question or only establishes that Locke is writing within the Christian natural law tradition, broadly construed, not that he was committed to Aristotelian essentialism.

In the fourth essay, for example, Locke turns to a discussion of the content of natural law and the manner in which it is made known. The law of nature, argues Locke, is known through reason and sense-experience. He further suggests that there is a connection between certain natural

---

[4] Samuel Zinaich Jr., *John Locke's Moral Revolution: From Natural Law to Moral Relativism* (Lanham: University Press of America, 2006), 70, note 11. All references to this text will be provided by page number within parentheses in the body of the text.

propensities shared by all human beings and the precepts of the natural law. As Locke observes:

> Further, he feels himself not only to be impelled by life's experience and pressing needs to procure and preserve a life in society with other men, but also to be urged to enter into society by a certain propensity of nature, and to be prepared for the maintenance of society by the gift of speech and through the intercourse of language, in fact as much as he is obliged to preserve himself (157, f. 61).

Zinaich compares this favorably with Thomas Aquinas' derivation of the order of natural law principles from the order of natural inclinations, and views this as further evidence of Locke's commitment to essentialism (39).

Despite the similarities between these two accounts, Locke's acceptance of the Thomistic account of natural inclinations is ambivalent at best. Locke does not so much infer a natural law principle from a specific natural inclination, as bring together a collection of observations about the human condition, including "life's experience and pressing needs," which provide the material basis for grasping a precept of the natural law. Moreover, when Locke has the opportunity to affirm that the natural law can be known by rational reflection on natural inclinations, he denies that this is the case. This denial is all the more mysterious in that it occurs only in the title of an unwritten essay, "Can the Law of Nature be Known from Man's Natural Inclinations? No," that Locke had added at the end of the fourth essay. Of course, there is no way of knowing why Locke never completed this essay, but Zinaich's suggestion that the essay would be redundant, merely repeating the denial that the natural law is inscribed (innate) in the minds of men contained in the third essay is unconvincing, since a natural inclination is not equivalent to an innate idea. Nevertheless, his explanatory comment, to the effect that there is no way to discriminate between the inclinations which dispose us to do our duty from those that lead us astray without "some sense of who God is," is more telling (73, note 37). This suggests that, in contrast with the assumptions underlying Aristotelian essentialism, Locke does not believe that rational reflection on human nature alone is sufficient to reveal the principles of natural law.

For Locke, it is not so much natural inclinations, but God's intentions for humanity that are the grounds for ascertaining our moral duties, and it is only by viewing these inclinations in the light of God's intentions, that they become meaningful.[5] Even though Aquinas would note that metaphysically the natural law is a subset of God's eternal law, he was careful to make the epistemic point that our human knowledge of natural law can only be based on our reflection on those natural inclinations that are essential to human nature, not on any appeals to our knowledge of the mind of God. For Aquinas, essentialism and a teleological understanding of nature is decisive for our ability to grasp the principles of natural law. This is not the case for Locke, where our knowledge of the natural law presupposes our understanding of the purposes ordained by God.

Locke's apparent reluctance to fully embrace essentialism and its implications for traditional natural law theory is reinforced by his clear and unwavering adherence to a moderate voluntarist theory of law—another clear departure from Thomas Aquinas' intellectualism. With this in mind, it is not surprising that Locke begins the first essay by asserting that that no one can deny the existence of God and that the natural order of things is ordained By God. He then describes the natural law as "the decree of the divine will discernible by the light of nature and indicating what is and what is not in conformity with rational nature, and for this very reason commending or prohibiting" (111, f. 11). Locke further explains that the natural law is "less correctly termed by some people the dictate of reason, since reason does not so much establish and pronounce this law of nature as search for it and discover it as a law enacted by a superior power and implanted in our hearts" (111, f. 12). By rejecting the claim that the natural law is best described as a "dictate of reason," Locke has moved away from the intellectualism of Thomas Aquinas toward a modified version of voluntarism, associated with Francisco Suárez, Nathanael Culverwel, and Samuel Pufendorf.

Zinaich's claim that Locke had a classical understanding of virtue and vice is based on the aforementioned essentialism, as well as his reading of Locke's fifth argument for the existence of natural law which states, in part, that "without natural law there would be neither virtue nor vice, neither reward of goodness nor the punishment of evil: there is no fault, no guilt, where there is no law" (119, f. 20). Since Locke never develops a theory of virtue, Zinaich assumes that if Locke did ground the natural law in an essentialist metaphysics then he must have grounded the distinction between virtue and vice in the same way. In fact, most of Zinaich's

---

[5] For further discussion of this point, see Ian Harris, *The Mind of John Locke: A Study of Political Theory in its Intellectual Setting* (Cambridge: Cambridge University Press, 1994), 98.

discussion of this point consists in an exposition of Aquinas' analysis of virtue, culminating in his statement that "all the acts of virtue are prescribed by the natural law" (43). But what stands out in Locke's comments on virtue is not the connection between natural law, natural inclinations, and virtue, as Zinaich suggests, but the connection Locke sees between law and virtue, that is, without law, which is the expression of superior's will, there can be no virtue nor vice, no reward and no punishment. Again, Locke's voluntarism, including the need for externally imposed sanctions, significantly shifts the focus of his attention away from human nature and its inclinations, as the source of law and virtue, to the divine will and God's power to reward and punish.

Zinaich concludes this chapter with an extensive analysis of Locke's discussion of natural law centered on establishing Locke's commitment to moral absolutism: the view that "there is a single, ultimate, moral standard, which is binding for all people at all times" (44). In the process Zinaich provides an excellent response to critics, like Zuckert[6] and Horowitz,[7] who inspired by the spirit of Leo Strauss, have sought to uncover the plethora of intentional inconsistencies and contradictions in the text which indicate Locke's secret alliance with Hobbes and his rejection of traditional natural law. Zinaich's care and meticulous attention to what Locke actually writes makes this one of the best sections of the book. Fortunately, his reconstructions of Locke's arguments can stand on their own, independent of his beliefs about Locke's reliance on Aristotelian essentialism.

After defending his traditional reading of the *Essays*, Zinaich turns to Locke's *Essay Concerning Human Understanding*. It is commonly assumed that Locke's *Essay* had its origins in a conversation among friends about the "principles of morality and revealed religion," more specifically, one of those friends, James Tyrell, noted that the discussion was about "the Law of Nature as the basis of morality and its implications for natural as well as revealed religion."[8] Put differently, Locke's goal in the *Essay* was to provide an epistemological foundation for our knowledge of natural law that he had begun in the *Essays*. Both texts

---

[6] Michael P. Zuckert, "On the Lockean Project of a Natural Law Theory: Reply to Zinaich," *Interpretation* 29, No. 1 (2001), 75-89.

[7] Robert Horowitz, "John Locke's Questions Concerning the Law of Nature," *Interpretation* 19, No. 3 (1992), 251-306.

[8] W. von Leyden, *Introduction to the Essays on the Law of Nature*, 9.

certainly reflect Locke's rejection of innate ideas and his efforts to ground knowledge on a combination of reason and sense-experience. This approach assumes that the two works are part of the same intellectual project.

In contrast, Zinaich argues that the *Essay* is primarily rooted in Locke's response to the "epistemological crisis" caused by the demise of Aristotelian essentialism and its replacement by the corpuscular theory of nature, especially as advocated by Robert Boyle. Zinaich takes for granted that the rejection of Aristotelian essentialism is tantamount to the rejection of natural law. His analysis of the *Essay* develops Locke's arguments accordingly. It is worth noting that these two goals are not necessarily incompatible. Locke could have been attempting to develop an understanding of natural law based on the new science, in which case the *Essay* can be construed as a continuation of the project begun in the *Essays*.[9]

After reviewing Locke's rejection of innate knowledge and his critique of the Scholastic view of essences, including an account of the distinction between nominal and real essences, Zinaich provides a detailed analysis Locke's moral relativism, which he assumes is grounded in the corpuscularian world-view. We can begin with Locke's doctrine of hedonism, for as Locke declares, "what has an aptness to produce *Pleasure* in us, is that we call *Good*, and what is apt to produce *Pain* in us, we call *Evil*, for no other reason, but for its aptness Pleasure and Pain in us, wherein consists our *Happiness* and *Misery*."[10] Zinaich correctly observes that Locke views our complex idea of good or evil as relation between persons who can feel pleasure or pain and objects which have the power to cause pleasure and pain (114). Zinaich also refers to this particular relation as a "conventional" relation, in order to capture the element of subjectivity typically inherent in such ideas, thereby exploiting Locke's claim that relations are voluntary collections of simple ideas, which the mind (partially) puts together, without any reference to any real archetypes, or standing patterns, existing anywhere (108). Put differently, in contrast with our ideas of substances, which intend to represent real

---

[9] See John Colman, *John Locke's Moral Philosophy* (Edinburgh: Edinburgh University Press, 1983), 240-242.

[10] John Locke, *An Essay Concerning Human Understanding*, edited by Peter H. Nidditch (Oxford: Clarendon Press, 1975), II.21.42. All references to this work will be provided within parentheses in the body of the text and listed by book, chapter, and paragraph.

things, our complex ideas of relations are to some degree dependent on the mind. In this case, at least, Locke acknowledges the relativism often associated with hedonism.

Zinaich then connects Locke's relational conception of good and evil to his understanding of moral good and evil. For whereas good and evil have been shown to be nothing but pleasure and pain, or that which produces pleasure and pain for the subject, moral good and evil, says Locke, is only "the Conformity or Disagreement of our voluntary Actions to some Law, whereby Good or Evil is drawn on us, from the Will and Power of the Law-maker; which Good and Evil, Pleasure and Pain, attending our observance, or breach of the Law, by the Decree of the Law-Maker, is that we call Reward and Punishment" (II.28.5). Since moral goodness is also a relation that exists between two things, viz. the voluntary action and a rule, and since moral relations are not created with the intention to represent something existing without us, Zinaich infers that such "conventional relations terminate and are ultimately founded on our simple ideas of sensation and reflection that the mind (partially) puts together, and are intended to denominate or clarify actions" (119). Zinaich further insists that, for Locke, "moral goodness and evil are largely created by us and imposed upon the world in the sense that it is a means of categorizing the world" (119). If some particular act is to be morally good or evil, it must meet two conditions. First, it must be shown that the voluntary action which was performed was either consistent or inconsistent with some rule, a rule determined either by God, the civil authority, or the moral community. Second, it must be shown that there is the possibility of pleasure or pain attending the observance or the breach of the rule, which can be imposed by the will of the lawmaker (120). Zinaich concludes that this conception of morality is inconsistent with the view that there is a single, ultimate, moral standard (121).

This conclusion rests on the assumption that Locke believes that there exists no rule or law that is independent of human contrivance, and the truth of this assumption depends on Zinaich's interpretation of Locke's discussion of the three kinds of moral law: the divine law, the civil law, and what Locke calls, the law of opinion or reputation (II.28.7). Zinaich insists that in the first edition of the *Essay*, "Locke clearly implies that the rules upon which moral goodness depends can be based on any one of the three that he mentions" (141). Moreover, Zinaich suggests that Locke never claims that the natural law is part and parcel of the divine law; in fact, Locke was often accused of reducing morality to the law of opinion.

Of course, Zinaich reminds the reader that, in response to these critiques, Locke sought to clarify these issues in later editions of the *Essay*. Specifically, Locke added that the divine law is "that law which God has set to the actions of men,—whether promulgated to them by the light of nature, or the voice of revelation." He further notes that the divine law is "the only true touchstone of moral rectitude" (II.28.7, 8).

Zinaich, of course, finds these additions highly suspect. He suggests that Locke initially conceived of the divine law as simply one of three kinds of law that can be used to measure moral goodness (142), and he rejects Locke's own explanation that his intention in the *Essay* was not to argue that these are the right sources, only that they are in fact the possible sources that men do use (141). However, to avoid further criticism, he adjusted the text of the *Essay* to conform to a more orthodox position (142). But, Zinaich objects that this commits Locke to two inconsistent positions: "a theistic absolutist view" about moral goodness and "a relationally-based" notion of morality (142). After considering a variety of possible resolutions of this dilemma, Zinaich argues that the most plausible solution is that although Locke recognized that moral relativism (as well as atheism), is a "natural consequence" of corpuscularism, Locke himself remained, "personally and philosophically," committed to theism and moral absolutism, a commitment that is evident from *The Reasonableness of Christianity* (143). Yet in spite of Locke's personal beliefs, Zinaich insists that given his goal of producing an epistemology compatible with the corpuscular philosophy of nature, Locke had in effect abandoned the "metaphysical machinery" necessary to support the existence of natural law (147).

Prior to the publication of the *Essays*, Locke's credentials as a natural law theorist rested, not so much on the Essay, but on his appeals to the law of nature in the *Second Treatise of Government*. In order to complete his discussion of Locke's intellectual development, Zinaich turns his attention to the *Second Treatise*. Zinaich provides two distinct arguments aimed at challenging Locke's apparent commitment to the natural law tradition. The first argument is based on the Strauss-inspired analysis advanced by Richard Cox in his *Locke on War and Peace*.[11] Cox undermines Locke's natural law credentials by arguing that Locke's account of the state of nature constitutes a radical departure from the account given by more orthodox theorists. As Zinaich explains Cox's argument, although Locke

---

[11] Richard Cox, *Locke on War and Peace* (Oxford: Clarendon Press, 1960).

begins the *Second Treatise* with a traditional description of the state of nature, that is, a state of relative peace and order, where basically rational and social individuals possess the fundamental dispositions to live according to the natural law, he progressively modifies this description, until it begins to resemble the state of war and anarchy described by Thomas Hobbes. In short, by giving two distinct accounts of the state of nature, Locke conceals his rejection of the traditional state of nature, and at the same time covertly signals his agreement with Hobbes' *bellum omnia contra omnes*. The second argument simply returns us to Zinaich's interpretation of Locke's intellectual development and the themes advanced in the *Essay*. If the goal of the Essay is to "work out the implications of the new science beginning from the presupposition of corpuscularism and the constraints it imposes on our knowledge of goodness and evil," and if Locke is intellectually consistent, then it follows that, "although he uses the term 'natural law' he is no longer committed to its existence" (169).

Professor Zinaich's interpretation of both the *Essay* and the *Second Treatise*, while often insightful, breaks little new ground. His Aristotelian reading of the *Essays on the Law of Nature* is quite provocative and does provide the basis for a coherent interpretation of Locke's views on the natural law. Yet, as I have suggested, not all of the pieces fit together as well as one would like. Since Locke was acquainted with Boyle during the writing of the *Essays*, it is reasonable to assume that he was already wrestling with the implications of the corpuscular understanding of nature.[12] This would account, at least in part, for his voluntarism and his reluctance to fully embrace essentialism, even in these early writings. On another point, however, I agree with Zinaich's assessment of Locke's inability to reconcile two disparate strains in his thought, that is, his unwavering devotion to the Christian moral tradition and his equally strong commitment to the new science and all that it might entail. Perhaps in this light, John Locke is the quintessential modern philosopher.

---

[12] Roger Woolhouse, *Locke: A Biography* (Cambridge: Cambridge University Press, 2007), 34-35.

REPORT

REPORT ON THE 29TH ANNUAL INTERNATIONAL MEETING
OF THE AMERICAN MARITAIN ASSOCIATION

"Philosophy and Vocation: Conditions for Renewal—
Commemorating Vatican II"
The Phoenix Park Hotel and the Catholic University of
America in Washington, D.C., October 13–16, 2006
Sponsored by: The Ecclesiastical Faculties at The Catholic
University of America and chaired by John P. Hittinger of the
Sacred Heart Major Seminary

When one hears the words "Vatican II" one often hears one of two responses. Either one may express that this was the time that the Catholic Church finally got with the times and opened wide its doors to modernity and the world or it was the time when the Church lost much of its identity and sold the store. This conference was about interpreting the Council and, in particular, the controversial Pastoral Constitution on the church in the modern world "Gaudium et Spes (7 Dec 1965)."

As might be expected, there was much discussion over the effectiveness of *Vatican II* and the aforementioned Constitution as to what it retained of the Church's mission and as to what it acceded to modern culture. The Sunday session with the postmodern Augustinian Thomist Tracey Rowland (John Paul II Institute for Marriage and Family, Melbourne), author of the now celebrated *Culture and the Thomist Tradition After Vatican II* was precisely on this point. Rowland maintained that theologians have adopted too much of the vocabulary of the modern world and so have lost much of their influence. For example, rather than talking about a "right" to life, one should be talking about the sacredness or the sanctity of human life. One should put the discussion in the framework of Christian theology rather than the vocabulary of secular society.

Often during the conference much of the discussion of how the Church should dialogue with the contemporary world revolved around various perceived dialectical principles inherent in human religious experience. There was the grace and nature colloqium that was carried on by David Schindler (*John Paul II Institute for Marriage and Family,*

Washington), and others, such as Stephen Long of the newly formed *Ave Maria University*, in a panel on Schlinder's seminal work, *Heart of the World*. They considered the issue of how much should human nature be thought of as autonomous and how much should this nature be seen as having been graced? How much may an omnipresent notion of grace endanger even the concept of humanity? Schlindler wanted to stress the idea that the human person was essentially a graced "creature" and really could not be understood apart from that. Long argued that, on the contrary, one had to have a notion of the nature without grace in order to make sense of the latter. Long said that he believes that Schindler's dual co-definition of nature and grace makes nature defective until filled by grace. For Long, grace is not something that the lack of which man would not be man.

There was the paper given by Joseph Koterski, S.J. (*Fordham University*) on "The Use of Philosophy in Catholic Social Teaching: The Case of *Gaudium et Spes*." He was considering the often perceived dualities between social justice and pure spirituality, and between the natural law tradition of St. Thomas and personalism. Koterski insisted that the human being can be known both through reason and in the light of faith. He argued that we should take a stereophonic approach and embrace both sides of these issues.

Christopher Cullen, S.J. (*Fordham University*) argued in "A New Benedict: Ratzinger and the Church in the Modern World" argued that the dualism between Church and State was important and that the origin of the dualism between the Sacred and Secular, the Church and the State, began with Christianity, with Jesus's "Render unto Caesar . . . "

James Schall S.J. in his "Maritain and the Intellectual Vocation" said that Maritain had claimed that we lived in two worlds: the world of things that are already there before us and the invisible world, and the latter is what is most important in the classroom. Even practical things exist only because there were invisible human capacities already there!

Many times philosophers and scientists make mistakes in their reasoning not because they reason poorly or have invalid arguments, but because their original concepts concerning human nature are flawed. Our concepts "need a good scrubbing" argued John Trapani Jr. (Walsh University) in his Mortimer Adlerian Style in his "Gate-Keeper of Small Mistakes: The Philosopher's 'Other' Vocation" paper. These cognitive mistakes such as those concerning happiness and pleasure stem from a faulty view of human nature.

Finally, if the concept of human nature is important to a notion of natural law, then the next presentation worthy of mention is something like a call to arms for the natural law theorist. Edmund Pellegrino, (*Georgetown University*) Chairman of the President's Council on Bioethics (see http://bioethicsprint.bioethics.gov/aboutpellegrino.html), gave a paper entitled "*Integral humanism* and the Crisis in Medicine," in which he argued that a philosophy of nature that includes a metaphysical notion of human nature is critical to protect ourselves from present and future abuses in the field of bioethics. In contemporary medicine, no longer does the idea of human dignity have any value and the dominant concept of man is that he is nothing more than the accidental combination of physics and chemistry. This results in a Hippocratic Oath that is disemboweled and where the ends of medicine are simply what we decide them to be. We need people to be a part of the current debate and dialogue.

At our banquet, Edmund Pellegrino received from the association the *Maritain Medal for Scholarly Excellence. The Humanitarian Award* was presented to Hamilton Reed Armstrong, internationally known sculptor (*Christendom College*) and the *Fides et Ratio: Lifetime Achievement Award* was presented to Jude P. Dougherty, Dean Emeritus, The School of Philosophy (*Catholic University of America*).

Other noteworthy papers were given by Michael Novak (American Enterprise Institute) on "Business as a Calling" and those given for the Annual *Gabriel Marcel Society* Meeting by Mr. Novak on "Marcel's Visit to America," by Brendan Sweetman (*Rockhurst*) on "Marcel and Postmodernism," by Sr. Prudence Allen, R.S.M. (*St. John Vianney Seminary*) on "Marcel and the Family," and by Timothy Weldon (*University of St. Francis*) on "Marcel and Mass Society."

The more recent (too late for discussion here) conference, the 30th Annual Convention, entitled "Nature, Science and Wisdom: The Role of the Philosophy of Nature" is/was held at Aquinas College and Loews Vanderbilt Hotel in Nashville, Tennessee from November 2nd to November 5th, 2006.

For further information about these international conferences or about the American Maritain Association please contact The American Maritain Association at the Jacques Maritain Center, 714 Hesburgh Library, Notre Dame, IN 46556. Tel: (574) 631-5825; E-mail: Alice.F.Osberger.1@nd.edu.

Gregory J. Kerr, Ph.D
DeSales University

ANNOTATED BIBLIOGRAPHY
OF RECENT WORKS IN NATURAL LAW
2000–2007

ANDERSEN, Svend, "Theological Ethics, Moral Philosophy, and Natural Law," *Ethical Theory & Moral Practice*; Dec 2001, Vol. 4, Issue 4, 349-364, 16p
[The article deals with the relationship between theological ethics and moral philosophy. The former is seen as a theoretical reflection on Christian ethics, the latter as one on secular ethics. The main questions asked are: (1) Is there one and only one pre-theoretical knowledge about acting rightly? (2) Does philosophy provide us with the theoretical framework for understanding both Christian and secular ethics? Both questions are answered in the negative. In the course of argument, four positions are presented: theological 'unificationism', philosophical 'unificationism', theological 'separationism' and Lutheran 'dualism'. It is argued that the latter position is most convincing. It is dual in the sense of being both a theory of Christian ethics and of including recognition of natural law. Hence, it unites a particularistic and a universalistic point of view. In the last section a reformulation of the Lutheran position is attempted in making use of the ethical theory of Knud E. Løgstrup's *The Ethical Demand*. (ABSTRACT FROM AUTHOR)
Reprinted with the permission of Springer Science & Business Media B.V.]

ARKES, Hadley, *Natural Rights and the Right to Choose*, (Book Review) *Ethics*; Jan 2005, Vol. 115, Issue 2, 435-436, 2p

ARNHART, Larry, "Darwinian Conservatism as the New Natural Law," *Good Society Journal*; 2003, Vol. 12, Issue 3, 14-19, 6p
[This article discusses the implications of Darwinian conservatism for the natural law. Foundation of conservatism on natural law; Description of the human biology of natural law; Assertion of

Thomas Hobbes that social and political order could arise only as an artificial construction of human reason.]

BELZ, Herman, "Americanization Of Natural Law: A Historical Perspective," *Good Society Journal*; 2003, Vol. 12, Issue 3, 7-13, 7p
[Discusses a historical dimension of the influence of the U.S. on natural law. Benefits of the human law for humans; Characteristics of natural law principles; Role of controversy over the relationship between natural law and natural rights in the articulation of ethical naturalism in modernity.]

BOYD, Craig A., "Participation Metaphysics in Aquinas's Theory of Natural Law," *American Catholic Philosophical Quarterly*: Journal of the American Catholic Philosophical Association; Summer 2005, Vol. 79, Issue 3, 431-445, 15p
[This article discusses philosophical issues concerning the theory of natural law of Saint Thomas Aquinas: Instance of theological definism; Ontology of natural kinds; important features of the theory; Consideration of the desire for God as a primary precept of the natural law.]

BOYD, Craig A., "Was Thomas Aquinas a Sociobiologist? Thomistic Natural Law, Rational Goods, and Sociobiology," *Zygon: Journal of Religion & Science*; Sep 2004, Vol. 39, Issue 3, 659-680, 22p
[Traditional Darwinian Theory presents two difficulties for Thomistic natural-law morality: relativism and essentialism. The sociobiology of E. O. Wilson seems to refute the idea of evolutionary relativism. Larry Arnhart has argued that Wilson's views on sociobiology can provide a scientific framework for Thomistic natural-law theory. However, in his attempt to reconcile Aquinas's views with Wilson's sociobiology, Arnhart fails to address a critical feature of Aquinas's ethics: the role of rational goods in natural law. Arnhart limits Aquinas's understanding of rationality to the Humean notion of economic rationality—that "reason is and ought to be the slave of the passions." On Aquinas's view, rationality discovers goods that transcend the merely biological, viz., the pursuit of truth, virtue, and God. I believe that Aquinas's natural-law morality is consistent with some accounts of sociobiology but not the more ontologically reductionist

versions like the one presented by Wilson and defended by Arnhart. Moreover, Aquinas's normative account of rationality is successful in refuting the challenges of evolutionary relativism as well as the reductionism found in most sociobiological approaches to ethics. (ABSTRACT FROM AUTHOR)]

BRENNER, William, "Natural Law, Motives, and Freedom of the Will," *Philosophical Investigations*; Jul 2001, Vol. 24, Issue 3, 246-261, 16p [Focuses on a Wittgensteinian view on natural law, motives and freedom of the will. Natural law and compulsion; Definition of unconscious motivation; Excerpt of an essay by Bertrand Russell on compulsion.]

BROWN, Vivienne, "Rights In Aristotle's Politics and Nicomachean Ethics?" *Review of Metaphysics*; Dec 2001, Vol. 55, Issue 2, 269-295, 27p, 1 chart [The article focuses on the significance of the individual natural rights concept in the political philosophy and ethics of Aristotle. Problems encountered in translating key Greek terms; Correlation between politics and natural rights; Accounts on the theoretical issues concerning the conceptions of political rights.]

BURNS, Tony, "Aquinas's Two Doctrines of Natural Law," *Political Studies*; Dec 2000, Vol. 48, Issue 5, 929-946, 18p [This paper examines the role which the concept of natural law has to play in the political thought of Aquinas, as this is to be found in the *Summa Theologiae*. It focuses particularly on Aquinas's understanding of the relationship which exists between natural and positive law. It argues that Aquinas's views are inconsistent and that the *Summa* actually contains two quite different positions regarding this subject. One of these is inherited from the Stoic natural law tradition and the other from Aristotle. The former considers natural law to be a critical standard by means of which positive law can be evaluated by individuals, whereas the latter does not. On the contrary, it maintains that according to Aquinas the principles of natural law require interpretation, and that this interpretation is to be provided, not by the conscience of the individual moral agent, but by positive law. Focus on either one or the other of these two documents leads to quite different interpretations of Aquinas's political thought as a whole. One such interpretation sees Aquinas as being a distant forerunner of the liberal political tradition. The other associates Aquinas much more closely with the notion of authority and hence with conservatism in politics. The article concludes by commenting on the relevance of these different interpretations of Aquinas for the contemporary debate between liberals and communitarians. (ABSTRACT FROM AUTHOR)]

BURNS, Tony, "Sophocles' *Antigone* and the History of the Concept of Natural Law," *Political Studies*; Aug 2002, Vol. 50, Issue 3, 545-557, 13p
[This paper focuses on two related questions. The first of these is a general question. Where are the origins of the concept of natural law to be located in the history of political thought? The second is more specific. Sophocles puts into the mouth of the eponymous heroine of his *Antigone* an argument justifying her disobedience to an edict of her uncle Creon, who forbade her to bury her brother Polyneices. Does this argument involve an appeal to the concept of natural law? The paper takes issue with the claim, first made by Aristotle in his *Rhetoric*, that Sophocles' *Antigone* is indeed an early example of the application of the concept of natural law in political argument and debate. This interpretation of the political message of the *Antigone* is inconsistent with what we know about Sophocles' attitude towards the fundamental questions of Athenian politics in the classical era of Periclean democracy during the fifth century BC. (ABSTRACT FROM AUTHOR)]

BUTTERWORTH, Charles, "On Natural Right and Other Unwritten Guides to Political Well-Being." *Good Society Journal*; 2006, Vol. 15, Issue 2, 53-55, 3p
[The author focuses on the relationship between natural right, natural law and other unwritten guides to political well-being. He agreed with Rene Descartes' explanation that clear and distinct reasoning leads to the truth and shows that there is no such thing as natural law. He believes in the existence of natural right, guided with the principles of Aristotle that reflected deeply on nature and how it can shape human conduct.]

COOPE, Christopher Miles, "New Natural Laws for Old," *Philosophical Quarterly*; Jan 2007, Vol. 57, Issue 226, 117-122, 6p
[Book Review of *Human Values: New Essays on Ethics and Natural Law*, edited by David S. Oderberg and Timothy Chappell.]

DEBRANANDER, Firmin, "Stoic Realpolitik," *International Philosophical Quarterly*; Sep 2006, Vol. 46, Issue 3, 277-292, 16p
[Thanks to its doctrines of natural right and moral egalitarianism and to its prominent historical role in defying totalitarian government, Stoicism is often cited as a touchstone for liberal democracy. Less well known, however, is an alternate lineage, culminating in a Stoic Realpolitik that emerges in Justus Lipsius's political writings. The foundation of this Realpolitik becomes increasingly clear in the progression of Stoic thought through Seneca, Epictetus, and Marcus Aurelius. Tracing this lineage reveals that the subject of politics is fundamentally problematic for Stoicism, especially since the denigration of politics is central to Stoic ethics. The Stoics ultimately arrive at a surprising moral pessimism, evidenced most prominently in Marcus's *Meditations*. In Lipsius's version of Stoic Realpolitik, the populace is characterized as being of inconstant behavior, and Stoicism is viewed as a resource for steeling the prince's character against the masses, whose moral emendation is hopeless. (ABSTRACT FROM AUTHOR)]

DIBLASI, Fulvio, "Natural Law and Natural Rights (Early Period)," *Continuum Encyclopedia of British Philosophy*; 2006, Vol. 3, 2301-2304, 4p
[Definitions of the terms "natural law" and "natural rights" are presented. The qualification 'natural' specifies that the source of normativity or value is more-than-human. Natural is opposed to 'conventional' as something that does not proceed from human free choice, but rather grounds and/or guides it.]

EPSTEIN, RICHARD, "The Not So Minimum Content of Natural Law," *Oxford Journal of Legal Studies*; Summer 2005, Vol. 25, Issue 2, 219-255, 37p
[This article examines Han's claim that it is possible to identify a core set of moral principles that constitute the minimum content of natural law. It argues that there is no reason to link natural law solely to self-preservation when its principles could be extended

to maximize social welfare. The article then shows how these so-called minimum rules of property, contract, and ton have in fact large generative powers that allow them to explain many of the salient features of any complete legal system. The article also shows how the relevant principles in this regard can be developed by an appeal to Hart's principles of defeasibility and causation. Both of these concepts organize the orderly and incremental expansion of legal rules from their initial core into a complete legal system. (ABSTRACT FROM AUTHOR)]

EZRA, Ovadia, Cherly Hughes and Andrew Light, "Human Rights: The Inapplicable Concept," *Social Philosophy Today*; 2004, Vol. 19, 217-235, 19p
[This paper seeks to ascertain the reasons for the regrettable gap between the extent to which human rights are acknowledged in many countries, and the extent to which residents of those countries in fact are able to enjoy these rights. However, when we seek to assess to what extent residents of those countries in fact enjoy these rights, the findings are somewhat depressing. In this paper I suggest an explanation for this phenomenon and argue that its cause is built into the very structure of Human Rights as these have hitherto been understood. I maintain that because the addressees of such rights are the states' governments, there is no external body that functions as the guarantor of such rights that has the authority and power to force the governments when they renege on their correlative duties as the addressees of Human Rights. (ABSTRACT FROM AUTHOR)]

FAN, Ruiping, "A Reconstructionist Confucian Account of Environmentalism: Toward a Human Sagely Dominion Over Nature," *Journal of Chinese Philosophy*; Mar 2005, Vol. 32, Issue 1, 105-122, 18p
[This article presents the Confucian view regarding environmental ethics, especially one that affords appropriate dominion of humans over nature. Assertions that Confucian view of the environment is often taken to be anthropocosmic rather than anthropocentric; Identification of three different possible senses of ethical anthro-pocentrism in order to clearly identify the Confucian view; Suggestion that principles are best understood as Confucian moral

requirements that reflect the virtue of supernatural personal power rather than the causal necessity of Daoist natural law.]

GAUTHIER, David, "Hobbes: The Laws of Nature," *Pacific Philosophical Quarterly*; Sep 2001, Vol. 82, Issue 3/4, 258-284, 26p
[Examines the law of nature by Thomas Hobbes. References to the laws of nature in the English version of *Leviathan*; Relation of civil law to the laws of nature; Characterizations of the laws of nature.]

GEORGE, Robert, *In Defense of Natural Law*, (Book Review) by Michael Menlowe, *Utilitas*; Mar 2005, Vol. 17, Issue 1, 119-121, 3p
[The article reviews the book *In Defense of Natural Law,* by Robert George.]

GEORGE, Robert, *Natural Law & Moral Inquiry: Ethics, Metaphysics & Politics in the Work of German Grisez*, (Book Review) by Philip Quinn, *Ethics*; Jan 2002, Vol. 112, Issue 2, 381-985, 4p
[Reviews the books *Natural Law and Moral Inquiry: Ethics, Metaphysics & Politics in the Work of Germain Grisez,* edited by Robert P. George, and *Common Truths: New Perspectives on Natural Law,* edited by Edward B. McLean.]

GOGGANS, Phillip, "Ethical Individualism and the Natural Law," *Ratio*; Mar 2000, Vol. 13, Issue 1, 28-36, 9p
["Generic qualities" are qualities typical of a kind because of the nature of that kind. It is commonly thought that generic qualities are morally irrelevant. For instance, the fact that human beings have a natural tendency to be thus-and-such is not relevant to moral acts involving a particular human being; what matters, rather, are the qualities of that individual. I argue that generic qualities are relevant in certain instances. First, we need to believe that this is so in order to be morally competent. Second, there is no other way to account for the rationality of the universal response to *Oedipus the King*. (ABSTRACT FROM AUTHOR)]

GÓMEZ-LOBO, Alfonso, *Morality and the Human Goods: An Introduction to Natural Law Ethics*, (Book Review) by Jonathan Sanford, *Review of Metaphysics*; Dec 2003, Vol. 57, Issue 2, 406-408, 2p [Reviews the book *Morality and the Human Goods: An Introduction to Natural Law Ethics*, by Alfonso Gómez-Lobo.]

GRABILL, Stephen J., *Rediscovering the Natural Law in Reformed Theological Ethics*, (Book Review) by Daniel B. Gallagher, *Renaissance Quarterly*; Fall 2007, Vol. 60, Issue 3, 940-941, 2p

GRIFFIOEN, A. L., "In Accordance with the Law: Reconciling Divine and Civil Law in Abelard," *American Catholic Philosophical Quarterly*: Journal of the American Catholic Philosophical Association; Spring 2007, Vol. 81, Issue 2, 307-321, 15p [The article discusses the philosopher Peter Abelard's view about a judge who knowingly convicts an innocent defendant in Great Britain. Abelard claims that the judge does rightly when he punishes the innocent man. Yet, the said claim of Abelard seems to be a counterintuitive to most people, however, the ethical system of Abelard cannot be viewed as completely subjective, since the rightness of an individual act of consent is grounded in objective standards established by God. A further examination for such subject basing Abelard's natural law, discoverable through reason, and the divine laws were explored to form an adequate civil law which would have to take under the judge and have acted rightly.]

HALL, Stephen, "The Persistent Spectre: Natural Law, International Order and the Limits of Legal Positivism," *European Journal of International Law*; 2001, Vol. 12, Issue 2, 269-307, 38p [International law was virtually synonymous with the natural law until the nineteenth century when the new doctrine of legal positivism supplanted Enlightenment naturalism as the dominant legal philosophy. Whereas the perennial jurisprudence of the natural law had conceived of the natural law and the positive law as complementary aspects of a single juridical reality, Enlightenment naturalism rejected or underestimated the role of positive law in regulating international relations. The confusion this error caused in international law rightly discredited Enlightenment naturalism. This did not, however, lead to a revival of older and more complete conceptions of the natural law. Austin's positivism expelled international law from the province of jurisprudence because it failed to conform to that theory's narrowly constructed definition of 'law'. Successive attempts by leading legal positivists to redeem international law for their school have led to a dilution of positivist doctrine, but have not furnished a coherent account of international law's juridical character. These revisions have failed to explain the persistence of non-positive juridical phenomena in the system, which may be highlighted by a detailed consideration of international law's sources. Legal positivism is also having an adverse impact on the theory and practice of international human rights law. (ABSTRACT FROM AUTHOR) *Reprinted with the permission of European Journal of International Law.*]

HEADLEY, John, "The Universalizing Principle and Process: On the West's Intrinsic Commitment to a Global Context," *Journal of World History*; Fall 2002, Vol. 13, Issue 2, 291-321, 31p
[The article focuses on the principle directed toward the construction of humanity as idea and fact to create the global arena for the realization of the universal jurisdiction of humanity during the Renaissance and Industrial period in Europe. Significance of the dualism of jurisdictions; Details of the development of later thinking upon natural law and natural rights during the sixteenth century; Difference among the three levels of civilizations. *Reprinted with the permission of University of Hawai`i Press.*]

HERBERT, Gary B. "On the Misconceived Genealogy of Human Rights," *Social Philosophy Today*; 2005, Vol. 21, 17-32, 16p
[The general practice of tracing the concept of human rights back to its presumed philosophical origins in the concepts of natural law and/or natural right, and invoking those concepts to give the idea of human rights its moral direction and philosophical substance, is dramatically mistaken. Interpreting human rights as the philosophical progeny of these earlier traditions allows the uglier aspects of natural rights and natural law, which the concept of human rights was intended to remedy, to serve as the defining characteristics of human rights. (ABSTRACT FROM AUTHOR) *Reprinted with the permission of Philosophy Documentation Center.*]

HOCHSTRASSER, T. J., *Natural Law Theories in the Early Enlightenment,*
(Book Review) by Steven Lestition, *Journal of Modern History*;
Mar 2004, Vol. 76, Issue 1, 162-165, 4p
[Reviews the book *Natural Law Theories in the Early Enlightenment,*
by T. J. Hochstrasser.]

HOEKSTRA, Kinch, "Hobbes on Law, Nature, and Reason," *Journal of
the History of Philosophy*; Jan 2003, Vol. 41, Issue 1, 111-120, 10p
[Studies the works of philosopher Thomas Hobbes regarding the
law of nature as a rule discovered by reason. Independence of the
moral psychology of Hobbes; Interpretation of the virtue of
reasoning.]

HUNTER, Ian and David Saunders, *Natural Law and Civil Sovereignty:
Moral Right and State Authority in Early Modern Political
Thought,* (Book Review) by Johann Sommerville, *Journal of
Ecclesiastical History*; Jul 2004, Vol. 55, Issue 3, 588-589, 2p
[Reviews the book *Natural Law and Civil Sovereignty: Moral
Right and State Authority in Early Modern Political Thought,*
edited by Ian Hunter and David Saunders.]

JACKSON, Bernard, "The Jewish View of Natural Law," *Journal of
Jewish Studies*; Spring 2001, Vol. 52, Issue 1, 136-146, 10p
[Presents the Jewish view of the natural law. Concept of Noahide
law; Ethical interpretation of scriptural norms; Secular version of
the law.]

KAINZ, Howard, *Natural Law: An Introduction and Re-Examination*, (Book
Review) by Raymond Dennehy, *Review of Metaphysics*; Dec 2005,
Vol. 59, Issue 2, 434-435, 2p
[The article reviews the book *Natural Law: An Introduction and
Re-Examination,* by Howard P. Kainz.]

KAINZ, Howard, "Reforming Natural Law," *First Things: A Monthly
Journal of Religion & Public Life*; Mar 2007, Issue 171, 4-4, 1/4p
[A letter to the editor is presented in response to the article "Protestants
and Natural Law," by J. Daryl Charles in the December 2006 issue.]

KING, Sallie, "From is to ought: Natural Law in Buddhadasa Bhikkhu and Phra Prayudh Payutto," *Journal of Religious Ethics*; Summer 2002, Vol. 30, Issue 2, 275-294, 19p
[The contemporary Thai Theravada Buddhist monks Buddhadasa Bhikkhu and Phra Prayyudh Payutto espouse a version of natural law thinking in which the norms of good behavior derive from the nature of the world, specifically its features of conditionality, causality, karma and interdependence. An ethic which stresses non-egoic harmony is the result. This paper (1) develops the notion of natural law in their thinking and (2) critically evaluates these ideas as a foundation for ethical thought, specifically asking whether such ideas recognize something of value in the individual per se and in individual freedom and, in an interdependent world, how one can challenge injustice or a brutal government. (ABSTRACT FROM AUTHOR)]

KOTERSKI, Joseph, "On the New Natural Law Theory," *Modern Age*; Fall 2000, Vol. 42, Issue 4, 415-419, 4p
[Reviews three books about natural law. *In Defense of Natural Law*, by Robert P. George; *Natural Law and Moral Inquiry: Ethics, Metaphysics, and Politics in the Work of Germain Grisez*, edited by Robert P. George; *Natural Law and Public Reason*, edited by Robert P. George and Christopher Wolfe.]

LANGE, Marc, *Natural Laws in Scientific Practice*, (Book Review) by John Carroll, *Philosophy & Phenomenological Research*; Jul 2005, Vol. 71, Issue 1, 240-245, 6p
[The article reviews the book *Natural Laws in Scientific Practice,* by Marc Lange.]

LANGLOIS, Anthony, "The Elusive Ontology of Human Rights," *Global Society: Journal of Interdisciplinary International Relations*; Jul 2004, Vol. 18, Issue 3, 243-261, 19p
[What are human rights? After looking at the reasons why the ontology of human rights should not be reduced to the human rights legal infrastructure, and noting that the origin of human rights in "natural law" is no longer a widely persuasive answer, I shall consider a number of recently popular alternatives. My purpose in examining these is to argue that the "what" of

human rights resides in philosophical claims about the value of the human person. The particular approaches considered all depend upon a "high anthropology." I argue that contemporary accounts take this high anthropology from historical sources they no longer think viable, without giving an alternative account of why it should be held. Such an account is necessary, however, for human rights to be an authoritative political doctrine. (ABSTRACT FROM AUTHOR)]

LEHOUX, Daryn, "Laws of Nature and Natural Laws," *Studies in History & Philosophy of Science Part A*; Dec 2006, Vol. 37, Issue 4, 527-549, 23p
[Abstract: The relationship between conceptions of law and conceptions of nature is a complex one, and proceeds on what appear to be two distinct fronts. On the one hand, we frequently talk of nature as being law-like or as obeying laws. On the other hand there are schools of philosophy that seek to justify ethics generally, or legal theory specifically, in conceptions of nature. Questions about the historical origins and development of claims that nature is law-like are generally treated as entirely distinct from the development of ethical natural law theories. By looking at the many intersections of law and nature in antiquity, this paper shows that such a sharp distinction is overly simplistic, and often relies crucially on the imposition of an artificial and anachronistic suppression of the role of gods or divinity in the worlds of ancient natural philosophy. Furthermore, by tightening up the terms of the debate, we see that the common claim that a conception of 'laws of nature' only emerges in the Scientific Revolution is built on a superficial reading of the ancient evidence.
Reprinted with the permission of Elsevier.]

LEWIS, V. BRADLEY, "Plato's Minos: the political and philosophical context of the problem of natural right. *Review of Metaphysics*; Sep 2006, Vol. 60, Issue 1, 17-53, 37p
[The article examines the political and philosophical context of natural law theory in the brief dialogue titled Minos. It is said that an inexplicit pronunciation of law as the first word in the dialogue could indicate ambiguity in the relationship between philosopher Socrates and his interlocutors. The comparison of law with stone and gold under the perspective of Socrates is cited.]

LLOYD, S.A., "Hobbes's Self-effacing Natural Law Theory," *Pacific Philosophical Quarterly*; Sep 2001, Vol. 82, Issue 3/4, 285-308, 24p [Examines the self-effacing natural law theory of Thomas Hobbes. Evidences on the positive conception of civil law; Essence of civil obedience in the law of nature; Consistency in defining civil law.]

MACIEJEWSKI, Jeffrey, "Natural Law as an Ethic for Postmodern Rhetoric," *International Journal of the Humanities*; Mar 2006, Vol. 3, Issue 7, 103-109, 8p [Although postmodern rhetorical theorists have held that rhetoric is a concomitant of human social life, they have seemingly been unable to identify a meta-ethical premise to warrant the moral directive that rhetoric must in some way be employed by individuals living in society. In this paper, I offer natural law ethical theory as one such philosophical foundation. I contend that insofar as reason makes possible the apprehension of our disposition to live with one another in society, so too does it undergird the use of rhetoric in motivating the will and precipitating action. Moreover, I assert that justice lends normative order to such endeavors, as it moderates the manner in which we live with one another in society. In view of this functional duality, I believe that natural law affords itself as an ethic for a postmodern conception of rhetoric. (ABSTRACT FROM AUTHOR)]

MACIEJEWSKI, Jeffrey and David T. Ozar, "Natural Law and the Right to Know in a Democracy," *Journal of Mass Media Ethics*; 2005, Vol. 20, Issue 2/3, 121-138, 18p [This article places the concept of "right to know," which is normally associated with law, in a moral framework. It outlines multiple meanings of the concept, emphasizing the institutional nature of "right to know." Then the article imbeds this understanding in moral thinking, including a discussion of the moral elements of rights, and applies that understanding in specific journalistic situations. (ABSTRACT FROM AUTHOR)]

MCLEAN, Edward, editor, "Common Truths: Natural Law and Moral Inquiry," (Book Review) by Philip Quinn, *Ethics*; Jan 2002, Vol. 112, Issue 2, 381-385, 4p

MUMFORD, Stephen, "Normative and Natural Laws" *Philosophy*; Apr 2000, Vol. 75, Issue 292, 265-283, 18p
[Examines the correlation between normative and natural laws. Advancement of prescriptivism about natural laws; Consideration of the natural law as an articulation of a putative law; Origin of the norm as a difficulty of the normative account; Presence of modal features of the normative law in the natural law.]

MURPHY, Mark C., *Natural Law and Practical Rationality*, (Book Review) by Daniel McInerny, *Review of Metaphysics*; Sep 2003, Vol. 57, Issue 1, 165-168, 3p
[Reviews the book *Natural Law and Practical Rationality*, by Mark C. Murphy]

NIEMEYER, Gerhart, "What Price 'Natural Law'?" *Logos: A Journal of Catholic Thought & Culture*; Spring 2007, Vol. 10, Issue 2, 126-142, 17p
[The article defines the concept of natural law. Natural law is a symbolic form of human consciousness which came with classical Greek philosophy. The Greek legacy of natural law is described. The role of enlightenment progressivism and revolutionary futurism in destroying history as a symbolic form of consciousness in daily life is discussed.]

NOVAK, David, Natural Law in Judaism, (Book Review) by Charles Mathewes, *University of Toronto Quarterly*; Winter 2000/2001, Vol. 70, Issue 1, 298-300, 3p
[The article reviews the book *Natural Law in Judaism*, by David Novak.]

NURI, Yurdusev, "Thomas Hobbes and International Relations: From Realism to Rationalism,"*Australian Journal of International Affairs*; Jun 2006, Vol. 60, Issue 2, 305- 321, 17p
[This article attempts to provide a correction to the exclusive realist interpretations of Thomas Hobbes. It makes the point that Hobbes is not as close to a realist understanding of international relations as has been prevalently held. Given Hobbes's conception of man and the state of nature, the formation of Leviathan and the law of nature, it is here argued that Hobbes gives us a perception of international relations which is not always conflictual and

comprises the adjustments of conflicting interests, leading to the possibility of alliances and cooperation in international relations.

OAKLEY, Francis, *Natural Law, Laws of Nature, Natural Rights: Continuity and Discontinuity the History of Ideas,* (Book Review) by Jean Porter, *Journal of Religion;* Jul 2007, Vol. 87, Issue 3, 456-457, 2p

PIERCE, Christine, *Immovable Laws, Irresistible Rights: Natural Law, Moral Rights, and Feminist Ethics,* (Book Review) by Lon Watson, *Ethics;* Jul 2004, Vol. 114, Issue 4, 862-862, 3/4p

PORTER, Jean, "A tradition of civility: the natural law as a tradition of moral inquiry," *Scottish Journal of Theology;* 2003, Vol. 56, Issue 1, 27-48, 22p
[We are accustomed to think of the natural law as being more or less equivalent to a universal morality, whether this is seen as grounded in nature in some general sense, or more specifically in the deliverances of practical reason. There is another way of approaching the natural law, however, according to which it is identified with a specific moral tradition which cannot be adequately understood apart from some account of its historical development and social location. This paper defends the latter approach. It precedes by way of an examination of one phase in the development of the natural law tradition, namely, its formulation as a systematic moral theology in the early scholastic period. Scholastic reflection on the natural law follows the pattern of a tradition-based form of moral reasoning, and even though the scholastics did not understand their moral reflections specifically in those terms, their concept of the natural law is congruent with a modern understanding of it as a tradition of inquiry. (ABSTRACT FROM AUTHOR)]

PORTER, Jean, Nature as Reason: A Thomistic Theory of the Natural Law, (Book Review) by Christopher Kaczor, *International Philosophical Quarterly;* Mar. 2006, Vol. 46, Issue 1, 121

RADBRUCH, Gustav, "Five Minutes of Legal Philosophy (1945)," *Oxford Journal of Legal Studies;* Spring 2006, Vol. 26, Issue 1, 13-15, 3p
[The article focuses on the view of lawyers on the validity of the law. State authorities can be of benefit to the people through the

law. Public benefit along with justice is an objective of the law. The principles of natural law or the law of reason are known to be weightier than any legal enactment.]

ROSSI, Enzo, "Natural Law," *Continuum Encyclopedia of British Philosophy*; 2006, Vol. 3, 2300-2301, 2p
[A definition of the term "natural law" is presented. It can refer to a position in moral theory, according to which there are objective moral norms which can be derived from our understanding of the natural order. The idea of the natural order as the source of the objective foundation for morality and law can be traced back to antiquity.] possibility of alliances and cooperation in international relations. (ABSTRACT FROM AUTHOR)]

RUHL, Lealle, "Natural Governance and the Governance of Nature: The Hazards of Natural Law Feminism," *Feminist Review*; Autumn 2000, Issue 66, 4-24, 21p
[This article examines the precepts of natural law feminism, and in exploring the writings of two Canadian feminists, Maureen McTeer and Louise Vandelac, examines how natural law feminism is deployed in debates about how to theorize reproduction. I contend that the natural law perspective obscures many issues worthy of feminist inquiry, and, perhaps more critically, eschews a discourse that emphasizes reproductive freedom in favour of one which has at its centre a largely unproblematized view of reproduction that follows a biologically driven script of conception, gestation, childbirth and mothering as inherently and necessarily connected. I argue that this stance is particularly evident in natural law feminist analyses of ecology and the regulation of new reproductive and genetic technologies. In both these areas, natural law feminism poses the central problem as one in which feminists must zealously protect the natural association between women and reproduction; in so doing, natural law feminists' gloss over the nature of this association. I suggest a reframing of the focus of debates on reproduction from what is natural and what is socially constructed to how we demarcate the two. (ABSTRACT FROM AUTHOR)]

SCHOCKENHOFF, Eberhard, *Natural Law And Human Dignity: Universal Ethics In An Historical World*, translated by Brian McNeil, (Book Review) by Mark Graham, *Theological Studies*; Dec 2004, Vol. 65, Issue 4, 880-882, 2p

[Schockenhoff's principal objective is to defend a version of natural law capable of grounding universal moral claims while simultaneously overcoming common objections to natural law theory. To this end, he devotes the first chapter to problems associated with natural law reasoning, and then in the next two chapters discusses at length tow of the most serious objections to natural law, relativism and historicism. Although these two chapters are preambles to his substantive case for natural law in the second half of the book, they are wide-ranging, informative, and serious attempts to reckon with major philosophical and theological movements that undermine universal moral claims.

Relativism, according to S., is nothing but a self-contradiction: to assert that morality is relative to specific cultures, a relativist unwittingly employs a universalism that regards moral statements as applicable across cultures. Absent this implicit universalism, a relativist could only make moral claims about his or her particular culture.

S. is far more sympathetic to historicism and agrees that historicity is an inescapable aspect of human existence. Yet historicity does not spell doom for natural law theory. Properly understood, historicity entails epistemological humility and openness to revision and development since every normative moral statement is necessarily accompanied by certain historical baggage that precludes a complete grasp of moral truth.

Following Thomas Aquinas, S. claims that there are various gradations of natural law principles corresponding to the order of natural human inclinations. First order principles, which seek to protect the goods indicated by the most pressing inclinations, are universal, admit of no exception, and seek to secure only the minimal conditions necessary for human existence, or the "absolute kernel" of human dignity (189). First order principles lead to two affirmations: there are rights possessed by every person at all times that may not be violated; and here are intrinsically evil actions that are defined as violations of these rights. In the latter category are grouped the intentional killing of innocent person, torture, rape, lying, and adultery. S., however, does not believe that masturbation, homosexual acts, sterilization, and artificial contraception should be designated as intrinsic evils.

S. realize that this rather thin notion of natural law and derivative goods fails to specify the contents of human flourishing, and he spends the next chapter discussing elements of the Judeo-Christian moral tradition and the particular ways that they transcend minimalist natural law claims and offer more specific guidance in various departments of human life.

The book is impressive in many respects. It is thorough and precise about the specific problems associated with natural law theory, and the chapters on relativism and historicism exhibit impressive erudition and insight. Few books on natural law grapple so extensively and fairly with objectors as does this one, and its responses are admirable in their breadth and depth.

There are some drawbacks to the book. Conspicuously absent is any discussion of evolutionary theory and its challenge to natural law theory. The reason why natural human inclinations possess normative moral import, according to a Thomistic account of natural law, is that they represent the ordering wisdom of God. If the natural inclinations are products of evolution occurring over millennia, however, and if the evolutionary process is correctly characterized as random and haphazard (which most evolutionary theorists claim), with no discernible divine direction involved, then the theological connection between the natural inclinations and divine providence is severed, and along with it any notion that the natural inclinations possess normative moral import. In my opinion, evolutionary theory strikes at the heart of a Thomistic account of natural law. It would have behooved S. to address this issue at length.

Another shortcoming is the opacity surrounding S.'s bifurcation of the moral sphere into two dimensions: natural law, which supports the indispensable minimum for human existence; and formal revelation, which grounds an ethic of perfection that encompasses far more aspects of human life. Throughout the book, S. wants to limit the sphere of natural law only to those issues that bear upon the necessary minimal conditions for human existence. Yet in his discussions of practical moral issues he consistently goes beyond this limitation and renders moral judgments on these issues, based on his notion of natural law, without considering relevant biblical material. Thus, I wonder whether his bifurcation is artificial, as well as how these two spheres relate in practice.

Despite these drawbacks, S. makes a number of valuable contributions to contemporary natural law theory. While the book is a demanding read, requiring considerable background in natural law theory, it is worth the effort.
Reprinted with the permission of Theological Studies.]

SEN, Amartya, *Elements of a Theory of Human Rights,* (Book Review) "Rights as Aspirations," *The Wilson Quarterly*; Winter 2005, Vol. 29, Issue 1, 97-99, 2p
[Never mind all those lofty pronouncements in America's Declaration of Independence, France's Declaration of the Rights of Man, and the United Nations' Universal Declaration of Human Rights. The idea that humans have rights without specific legislation giving the rights legal definition and force is just "nonsense upon stilts," utilitarian philosopher Jeremy Bentham (1748–1832) asserted—and many modern thinkers agree. But Nobel laureate Sen, an economist at Harvard University, takes an opposing view.

Human rights are "primarily ethical demands," he says. Though they often inspire legislation, they're not mainly legal commands. They derive their importance from the underlying freedoms that they're about. "For example, the human right of not being tortured springs from the importance of freedom from torture for all." And the ethical demand is not just for the would-be torturer to desist, but for other persons to consider how torture can be prevented and what they themselves should reasonably do toward that end.

Bentham regarded natural rights as false legal pretensions. A modern law-centered view that's more accepting of the idea of human rights sees them as "laws in waiting." But for Sen, human rights are not just the basis for new legislation; they can also influence public opinion and prompt agitation on their behalf. In monitoring abuses of human rights, for example, Amnesty International and other watchdog groups promote the cause of human rights.

Only a freedom important enough to justify obliging other people to consider what they can do to advance it can become the basis for a human right, Sen maintains. And those other people must plausibly be able to make a difference.

Some contemporary thinkers accept the general idea of human rights but reject the inclusion of so-called economic and social rights, such as a common entitlement to subsistence or health care, because the institutions needed to fulfill those rights may not yet exist in many societies. But this, Sen argues, only indicates the need to work toward changing the circumstances that prevent such rights from being realized.

The ultimate test of the validity of claimed human rights, he says, is whether they survive uninhibited, informed discussion and scrutiny, not merely in one society but "across national boundaries." As Adam Smith once wrote, ethical scrutiny requires examining moral beliefs from "a certain distance."
Reprinted with permission from The Wilson Quarterly, Winter 2005. Copyright © 2005 by The Woodrow Wilson International Center for Scholars]

SIMON, Stephen, "Natural Law Reasoning and American Constitutional Discourse," *Good Society Journal*; 2003, Vol. 12, Issue 3, 27-31, 5p [This article discusses natural law reasoning and constitutional discourse in the U.S. Distinction of political rights from ordinary political considerations; Importance of the language and framework within which constitutional debate takes place; Adoption of the design of American constitutionalism.]

SORENSON, Leonard, "Rousseau's fulfillment of the natural public law tradition and his contribution to its demise," *European Legacy*; Aug 2005, Vol. 10, Issue 5, 439-454, 16p
[The recent research of Helena Rosenblatt, Hilail Gildin, Arthur Meltzer, and John Scott calls for a reconsideration of Rousseau's stance towards and effect on the natural public law tradition. This reconsideration is especially called for given the persuasive evidence and arguments that these scholars marshal to demonstrate the positive contribution of Rousseau to that tradition and to suggest that his pre-Kantian rational law teaching in the Social Contract is rooted in his post-Hobbesian stance towards natural law, especially in the Second Discourse. The work of these scholars builds upon others, especially on Leo Strauss, Victor Gourevitch, Jean Starobinski, Marc Plattner, Roger Masters and John Charvet, as well as Asher Horowitz, R. A. Leigh, Franz Haymann, and Robert Derathe, and completes the full range of alternative answers to our question. Their contributions are invaluable scaffolding for fully grasping the issue and for proposing theses that could resolve it. Given the great debt owed to these scholars, the present inquiry begins with an overview and general assessment of their opinions on the issue, which is then followed by a close analysis of the relevant texts of Rousseau, especially the "Preface" to the Second Discourse. (ABSTRACT FROM AUTHOR)]

STEIN, Peter, "The *ius commune* and its demise," *Journal of Legal History*; Aug 2004, Vol. 25, Issue 2, 161-167, 7p
[An amalgam of Roman law and canon law, the *ius commune* was developed in the university law faculties. Their traditional Bartolist approach to the texts was challenged by the French humanists and by the end of the sixteenth century humanism was accepted by diehards such as Gentili. Hugo Donellus conceived of law as a set of subjective rights to be distinguished from the remedies which enforced them. The *ius commune* declined with the growth of natural law and of the codification movement as well as the abandonment of Latin in favour of the vernacular in university teaching. (ABSTRACT FROM AUTHOR)]

STEVEN, Andrew, "Property Law and Human Rights," *Juridical Review*; 2005, Vol. 2005, Issue 4, 293-310, 16p
[This article considers the impact which the European Convention on Human Rights has had on Scottish properly law in its first five years of direct enforceability. It begins by giving an overview of domestic human rights legislation, with an examination of the difficult question of the extent to which the Convention has horizontal effect. There follows a discussion of Art. 1, Protocol i—the provision in the Convention which protects property rights. Thereafter, the effect of this provision on existing Scottish law and new legislation is considered. The conclusion drawn is that the impact has been more apparent as regards the latter than the former. (ABSTRACT FROM AUTHOR)]

TIERNY, Brain, "Permissive Natural Law and Property: Gratian to Kant," *Journal of the History of Ideas*; Jul 2001, Vol. 62, Issue 3, 381-399, 19p
[Focuses on natural law and property. Kantian argumentation on the theory of property; Universal law of Right by philosopher Immanuel Kant; Contrariness between personal possessions and natural law.]

TRAINA, Cristina, *Feminist Ethics And Natural Law*, (Book Review) by Patricia Beattie Jung, *Theological Studies*; Dec 2000, Vol. 61, Issue 4, 780-783, 3p
[Reviews the book `Feminist Ethics and Natural Law: The End of the Anathemas,' by Cristina L.H. Traina.]

VANDRUNEN, David, "Medieval Natural Law and the Reformation: A Comparison of Aquinas and Calvin," *American Catholic Philosophical Quarterly*: Journal of the American Catholic Philosophical Association; Winter 2006, Vol. 80, Issue 1, p77-98, 22p
[The article examines theologian John Calvin's ideas on natural law doctrine in comparison with those of theologian Thomas Aquinas. The author argues that significant points of both similarity and difference between them must be recognized. Striking similarities are their grounding of natural law in the divine nature and the relationship of natural to civil law. Differences include issues of participation, conscience and the two kingdoms doctrine.]

VAN DUFFEL, Siegfried, "How to Study Human Rights and Culture . . . Without Becoming a Relativist," *Philosophy in the Contemporary World*; Fall/Winter2004, Vol. 11, Issue 2, 88-95, 7p
[The article focuses on understanding the idea of human rights and culture. Relation between a culture and a doctrine; General description of the culture that is supposed to lack the concept of human rights; Investigation of the relation between the idea of human rights and a supposed individualism in western culture.]

WHITELEY, Patrick, "Natural Law and the Problem of Certainty," *Contemporary Literature*; Winter 2002, Vol. 43, Issue 4, 760-783, 24p
[Discusses how the play by Robert Bolt, *A Man for All Seasons*, puts the debate over natural law theory into contemporary context. Question of whether natural law is irreconcilable with legal positivism; whether natural law theory comports with moral relativism; Comparisons with Sophocles' *Antigone*.]

WOLFE, Christopher, *Natural Law Liberalism*, (Book), reviewed by, Groarke, Paul, *Heythrop Journal*; Nov 2007, Vol. 48, Issue 6, 1024-1026, 3p

YIN, Jing, "The Clash of Rights: A Critical Analysis of News Discourse On Human Rights In The United States And China," *Critical Discourse Studies*; Apr 2007, Vol. 4, Issue 1, 75-94, 20p
[This article examines the discursive strategies of news reports on China's human rights in *The New York Times* and *People's Daily*. After an analysis of local semantics, I argue that the discursive representations in the two newspapers reflect the struggle over articulation of human rights. *The New York Times* attempts to project the notion of natural rights as universal truth, whereas *People's Daily* defines human rights as a process of development to counter Western condemnation as well as to justify rights abuses in China. The struggle over articulation is also a manifestation of the hierarchy of discourse. The powerful try to fix the preferred meaning while the powerless strive to negate the dominant meaning. (ABSTRACT FROM AUTHOR)]

Contributors

Peter P. Cvek is chair of the Department of Philosophy at Saint Peter's College, Jersey City, NJ

Jacob M. Held is Assistant Professor of Philosophy at the University of Central Arkansas. He has published on punishment, gay marriage, and various other applied ethical problems. He is currently working on problems in Marxist ethics and theories of recognition, as well as moral philosophy and redemption. He is co-editor of *James Bond and Philosophy: Questions are Forever*, as well as a contributor to several other volumes in both *Open Court* and Blackwell's *Philosophy and Popular Culture* series.

Tibor Machan holds the R. C. Hoiles Chair in Business Ethics and Free Enterprise, Argyros School of Business & Economics, Chapman University, Orange, CA 92866.

Timothy D. Sullivan is an independent scholar living in Ohio, whose current research interest is the ethics of money on which he has authored a number of papers.

Francesco Viola is Ordinary Professor of Philosophy of Law in the Dipartmento di studi su Politica, Diritto e Societa at the University of Palermo, ITALY.

AUTHOR INDEX TO ARTICLES AND REVIEWS
VERA LEX NEW SERIES

VOLUME 1 (WINTER 2000) TO VOLUME 7 (WINTER 2006)

CALL FOR PAPERS ON
JUST WAR THEORY AND IRAQ

As the carnage in Iraq escalates out of control of the occupying military forces with no end in sight, and with increasing evidence of the imminent decline of the country into chaos, it is time to reevaluate United States war policy in relation to Just War Theory and the U.S. involvement in Iraq (*jus ad bellum* and *jus in bello*.) Since the conflict in Iraq has been going on for some time preference will be given to papers about *jus in bello*, although topics on *jus ad bellum* will be considered, as will general questions as to the relevancy of just war theory in a global environment.

In general the issues and questions are well-known, but much has changed in the way of information since the pre-emptive attack that requires a renewed inquiry. For example, it is widely believed that Iraq did not possess weapons of mass destruction and that the Bush administration fabricated evidence to the contrary; the execution of Saddam Hussein; definitive proof of torture at Abu Ghraib, and alleged torture at Guantánamo and other secret detention centers; mercenary combatants targeting non-combatants; the role of the U.S. government in post-conflict regime change . . .

Can these instances and, in all likelihood, the many others to follow, stand the test of just cause, comparative justice, legitimate authority, right intention, probability of success, proportionality (of harm to perceived good), and last resort? Regarding conduct in war (*jus in bello*), were the principles of discrimination, proportionality, minimal force adhered to; and what of torture, and respect?

All submissions should be sent by email attachment to Robert Chapman, Editor, at rchapman@pace.edu.

A small number of back copies of VERA LEX remain at a cost of USD $10.00 a copy.* A complete back set of VERA LEX is $115.00 (see list below). Those who order will receive, without charge, all five previous *graphically reproduced* issues neatly bound: Vol. 1, No. 1 (1979) through Vol. III, No. 1 (1982). [Vol. II No. 2 was not issued.] For more information on Pace titles, please visit the website: *http://www.pace.edu/press*

1982 Vol. III,	No. 2	**Reason in the Natural Law**
1986 Vol. VI,	No. 1	**Edmund Burke and the Natural Law: Theory and Practice**
	No. 2	**Is There a Natural Law in Hebrew Tradition?**
1987 Vol. VII,	No. 1	**Natural Law and Constitutionalism**
	No. 2	**Natural Law and Constitutionalism II**
1988 Vol. VIII,	No. 1	**Rights I**
	No. 2	**Rights II**
1989 Vol. IX,	No. 1	**(General Interest)**
	No. 2	**The Spanish Tradition** (Index: Yves R. Simon)
1990 Vol. X,	No. 1	**Thomas Aquinas**
	No. 2	**(General Interest)**
1991 Vol. XI,	No. 1	**Equity as Natural Law**
	No. 2	**Sacred and Secular Natural Law**
1992 Vol. XII,	No. 1	**Jurisprudence and the Natural Law**
	No. 2	**Legal Positivism, Pragmatism**

1993 Vol. XIII,   **Dignity as Natural Law**
Nos. 1&2 (double issue) (Rosmini, Trigeaud)

1994 Vol. XIV,   **Empirical Natural Law, Human Nature, Science**
Nos. 1&2 (double issue)

1995 Vol. XV,   **Autonomy, Independence, Liberty**
Nos. 1&2 (double issue)   (Includes 6-year cumulative index: 1990–1995)

2000 New Series Vol. I Nos. 1&2 (double issue)	**Natural Law and Natural Environment** (available direct from Pace UP)
2001 New Series Vol. II Nos. 1&2 (double issue)	**Liberalism and Natural Law** (available direct from Pace UP)
2002 New Series Vol. III Nos. 1&2 (double issue)	**Globalism and Natural Law** (available direct from Pace UP)
2003 New Series Vol. IV Nos. 1&2 (double issue)	**Feminism and Natural Law** (available direct from Pace UP)
2004 New Series Vol. V Nos. 1&2 (double issue)	**Medieval Natural Law Theories** (available direct from Pace UP)
2005 New Series Vol. VI Nos. 1&2 (double issue)	**The Work of John Finnis** (available direct from Pace UP)
2006 New Series Vol. VII Nos. 1&2 (double issue)	**Natural Law Theory & Asian Thought** (available direct from Pace UP)

*Two back issues of VERA LEX are out of print. However, the originals are available in <u>xeroxed</u> form for USD \$5.00.

1983–84 Vol. IV, Nos. 1&2 (double issue)	**Hugo Grotius** (index)
1985 Vol. V No. 1 (No. 2 was not issued.)	**Giambattista Vico**

Environmental Values

EDITOR:
Alan Holland
Dept. of Philosophy, Furness Coll.,
Lancaster University, LA1 1YG, UK

ASSOCIATED EDITORS:
Michael Hammond
Lancaster University
Robin Grove-White
Lancaster University
John Proops
University of Keele

REVIEWS EDITORS:
Clive Spash
University of Cambridge
Jeremy Roxbee-Cox
Lancaster University

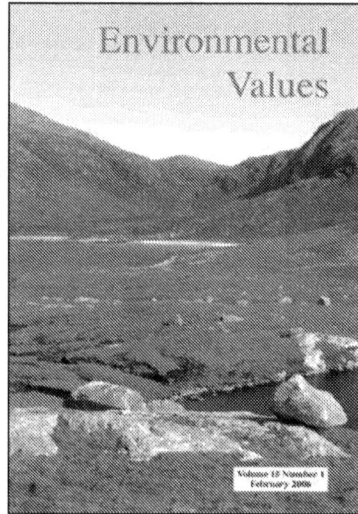

ENVIRONMENTAL VALUES is concerned with the basis and justification of environmental policy. It aims to bring together contributions from philosophy, law, economics and other disciplines, which relate to the present and future environment of humans and other species; and to clarify the relationship between practical policy issues and more fundamental underlying principles or assumptions.

The White Horse Press, 10 High Street, Knapwell, Cambridge CB3 8NR, UK
ISSN: 0963-2719 Quarterly (February, May, August, November)
Vol. 9, 2000, 144 pages per issue. Includes annual index.

Institutions: (1 year) £96 ($155 US)

(Institutional Rate Includes ELECTRONIC ACCESS)

Individual (1 year) £40 ($65 US)

Student/unwaged (1 year) £30 ($50 US)

Official Journal of the International Association for
Environmental Philosophy

Environmental Philosophy

$40 ($25 for students) annually with membership to International
Association for Environmental Philosophy

$25 individual non-membership subscription

Send payment to:
Kenneth Maly
Department of Philosophy
University of Wisconsin-LaCrosse,
LaCrosse, WI 54601

Published by the International Association for Environmental Philosophy, the University
of Wisconsin-LaCrosse and the Division of the Environment, University of Toronto

www.ingramcontent.com/pod-product-compliance
Lightning Source LLC
Chambersburg PA
CBHW071135280326
41935CB00010B/1232